Nursing: Art and Science

Nursing: Art and Science

Edited by

ALISON KITSON

RCN Standards of Care Programme,
Institute of Nursing,
Radcliffe Infirmary, Oxford

CHAPMAN & HALL

London · Glasgow · New York · Tokyo · Melbourne · Madras

Published by Chapman & Hall, 2–6 Boundary Row, London SE1 8HN

Chapman & Hall, 2–6 Boundary Row, London SE1 8HN, UK

Blackie Academic & Professional, Wester Cleddens Road,
Bishopbriggs, Glasgow G64 2NZ, UK

Chapman & Hall, 29 West 35th Street, New York NY10001, USA

Chapman & Hall Japan, Thomson Publishing Japan, Hirakawacho Nemoto
Building, 7F, 1–7–11 Hirakawa-cho, Chiyoda-ku, Tokyo 102, Japan

Chapman & Hall Australia, Thomson Nelson Australia, 102 Dodds Street,
South Melbourne, Victoria 3205, Australia

Chapman & Hall India, R. Seshadri, 32 Second Main Road, CIT East,
Madras 600 035, India

Distributed in the USA and Canada by Singular Publishing Group Inc.,
4284 41st Street, San Diego, California 92105

© 1993 Chapman & Hall

Typeset in Palatino by ROM-Data Corporation Ltd, Cornwall, England
Printed in Great Britain by Hartnolls Ltd, Bodmin, Cornwall

ISBN 0 412 47070 5   1 56593 063 0 (USA)

A catalogue record for this book is available from the British Library

Library of Congress Cataloging-in-Publication data
Nursing: art and science/edited by Alison Kitson
        p.   cm.
   Includes index.
   ISBN 1–56593–063–0
   1. Nursing–Philosophy–Congresses. 2. Nursing–Social aspects–
Congresses. 3. Nursing–Research–Congresses. I. Kitson, Alison L.,
1956–
RT84.5.N85 1992
610.73–dc20   92-32252
                                                          CIP

∞ Printed on permanent acid-free text paper, manufactured in
accordance with the proposed ANSI/NISO Z 39.48-199X and ANSI Z
39.48-1984

Contents

Contributors

Agnes Bjorn   MPhil PhD Registered Nurse and Nurse Teacher. Director of the Danish Institute for Health and Nursing Research, and programme manager in the WHO/EURO study on People's Needs for Nursing Care (1980–9). Present post: reader in Health Care Studies, Oxford Polytechnic.

Senga Bond   PhD RGN FRCN is one of three co-directors of the Centre for Health Services Research at the University of Newcastle upon Tyne. She is currently a member of the editorial boards of the *Journal of Advanced Nursing* and the *International Journal of Nursing Research*, and a member of the Medical Research Council Health Services Research Committee. Her current research interests are devoted to evaluating health services in general and nursing in particular, with an emphasis on measures of outcome.

Gillian Dalley   was a Research Fellow at the Policy Studies Institute. She has recently taken up a managerial appointment with South East Thames Regional Health Authority. Earlier in her career she worked for the King's Fund and the Centre for Health Economics of York. Her main interests are community care and quality in health and social care.

Len Doyal   is Senior Lecturer in Medical Ethics at St Bartholomew's and the London Hospital Medical Colleges, the first appointment of its kind in the United Kingdom. As Principal Lecturer in Philosophy at Middlesex Polytechnic, he taught for over 20 years after coming here from the United States on a Fulbright Scholarship to study with Karl Popper at the London School of Economics. He has published widely in the philosophy of science and moral and political philosophy, including *Empiricism, Explanation and Rationality: An Introduction to the Philosophy of the Social Sciences* (with Roger Harris) and *A Theory of Human Need* (with Ian Gough).

Alastair Gray   is an economist with particular interests in the health care sector and the nursing labour force. He is currently working on a detailed study of nursing turnover and local labour markets. He has acted as an adviser to the World Health Organisation on the economics of nursing, and has written on economic aspects of nursing in a range of journals, monographs and books. He was a member of the team which produced the Open University course *Health and Disease*, and is now involved in revising the course textbooks and reader.

Alison Kitson is Director of the Royal College of Nursing Standards of Care Programme and of the Institute of Nursing in Oxford. She is associate editor of the *Quality in Health Care* journal and has been a consultant for WHO on quality assurance. She is a Fellow of the Royal College of Nursing and holds a personal chair at Oxford Polytechnic.

Kath Melia Following graduation from Manchester University, Department of Social and Preventive Medicine, she worked in intensive care before joining a research team at the Nursing Studies Research Unit at Edinburgh University in 1975. Research interests include the sociology of occupations, with a particular interest in the occupational changes taking place within nursing, qualitative research methods and nursing health care ethics.

Anne-Marie Rafferty Anne-Marie lectures to undergraduate and master's students in nursing and teaches research methods to post-registration nurses. She tutors nursing and medical students in basic epidemiology and agricultural science students in the sociology of science. She has undertaken clinical research into postoperative backache in hospitalized patients, and has recently completed her doctoral dissertation on the politics of nursing education, 1860–1948. Anne-Marie is currently researching leadership in nursing.

Jane Robinson is Professor and Head of the Department of Nursing Studies at the University of Nottingham. She is an orthopaedic and general trained nurse, a health visitor and health visitor tutor. Her research interests lie in policy analysis in relation to women, and women as nurses.

Christine Webb BA, MSc, PhD, SRN, RSCN, RNT is Professor of Nursing at the University of Manchester. She trained as a general and sick children's nurse in London, then took a degree in sociology at Manchester University. Following posts as a night sister and gynaecology ward sister, she became a nurse tutor. Having worked in Mozambique for 3 years as a nurse tutor, she returned to this country as a senior nurse tutor and studied part-time for a master's degree in the sociology of education. There followed 2 years as a research assistant on a project examining recovery from hysterectomy, for which she was awarded a PhD. She then lectured at Manchester University in nursing for 18 months, then moved to Bristol Polytechnic as Principal Lecturer in Nursing to set up full-time and part-time degrees in nursing. Research interests: women's health, theory and practice of nursing, action research.

Introduction

The papers making up the contents of this book were presented at a seminar series hosted by the Institute of Nursing in Oxford. The purpose of the series was to encourage an invited audience of practising nurses, academics and researchers to get together to discuss and critically analyse some of the things we tend to take for granted in nursing. While such events are becoming more and more commonplace, we felt there was a need to publish the papers themselves, along with summaries of the discussions that followed, for a number of reasons.

First, the quality of the papers themselves merits wider dissemination than to a group of 30 people. Second, the structure of the series attempted to guide the group – and the reader – through a logical journey of discovery, beginning with broad philosophical issues relating to the nature and form of knowledge through to a series of presentations on the strengths and weakness of particular types of research methodologies used in nursing. But perhaps the main reason is because of the quality of the debate that followed the papers. Even though this can be captured only rather inadequately in the present text, the key themes that emerged from each discussion illustrate both the level and the nature of debate required to understand some of the complex issues facing nursing today.

A series title as overbearing as 'Nursing: Art and Science' undoubtedly disappoints some and frustrates others. Indeed, the idea of trying to cover such an amount of intellectual territory is at best foolhardy and at worst academic suicide. But what was very encouraging was the way in which key themes began to emerge early on, and then kept re-emerging. Central to all of the papers was the acknowledgement, either implicit or clearly stated, of the need to view nursing knowledge as profoundly influenced by the social context within which nursing is practised. This was stated categorically in Jane Robinson's paper, where she exhorts nurses to break free from the intellectual bondage implied by using inappropriate theories, models and analogies from the natural sciences, and become more confident in engaging in careful descriptions of nursing intervention using more appropriate social investigation techniques.

Melia takes this debate forward in her paper by suggesting that the issue (in nursing) no longer rests on the merits or demerits of the qualitative/quantitative approach. Rather, the central questions are what do we want to know and how best might we find it out? She goes on to say that if the question rests within the physical world (that pertaining to the natural sciences) the answer is theoretically more likely to be straightforward, although technically complex. Conversely, if the question is dealing with the social world, then as Melia states, the operational means by which we link our conceptual notions of the phenomena under study to the empirical data available is problematic.

Both Bond's and Webb's contributions illustrate the limitations and strengths of other research methodologies, namely the experimental approach and action research. The overriding concern identified in both papers, but particularly in Bond's, relate to the robustness of the use of the particular method. Sloppy research approaches, with the contravention of some of the most basic research rules, were all too common occurrences in her experience and should be avoided at every stage, no matter what methodology was chosen.

The relationship between the generation of nursing knowledge and health policy formulation was another theme that ran through the series. Robinson described the lack of nursing contribution to any major health policy decisions at health authority level, as reflecting the 'Black Hole Theory of Nursing' and proposed ways of getting out of it. In contrast, Dalley focused on a particular health policy – that of community care – and cleverly illustrated how that policy was derived not from any well-thought-out rational argument, but from a number of opinions and prejudices of key individuals who held on to old-fashioned notions of the role of the family and women in society. Her solution to this, not unlike that advocated by Robinson, was to ensure that alternative solutions to the problem were presented and heard in the right places.

The issue of having one's views or concerns represented came up time and time again, not only in terms of nursing concerns but also relating to patients. Doyal started the debate by suggesting that, despite the shared view that knowledge is context-related, there do exist a number of universal truths which are independent of context. In Doyal's view, these universals comprise the application of certain technological knowledge; the meeting of key basic human needs such as health and wellbeing; and acknowledging individual rights such as freedom and autonomy. Are such universal requirements indeed independent of social context and culture? And if so, what sort of personal, professional and political tensions do such beliefs create in people who have to act and care for others? Or is it easier for us to accept the gospel of relativism?

An interesting contrast to Doyal's view was put forward by economist Alastair Gray, who suggested that need is relatively useless as a concept in trying to understand how a nursing service can be delivered equitably. His clear presentation of the numbers of nurses in EEC countries being more closely linked to gross national product (GNP) figures than anything to do with identified health needs of the community is a chastening reminder of the complex interconnections between knowledge, theory, policy, research and politics.

The role of women in society was a topic which, unsurprisingly, emerged with almost monotonous regularity. Both Kitson's and Rafferty's papers considered the effects of the traditional images of nursing and caring on the concepts and models that are used to describe nursing and its sociopolitical activities. Not only was there historical consistency in the issues that tended to arise, but, as illustrated in Bjorn's paper, the similarities did not stop at the English channel. Throughout Europe, nursing seemed to be facing a very similar challenge, according to Bjorn's observations.

Even the casual reader of this text will be struck by the areas of convergence in the papers, and most interestingly by the strongly held opposing perspectives of some. Each contribution comes with its own biased, prejudiced view of the world, substantiated by experience, interpretation and so-called evidence to support one view rather than another. What is vitally important to the reader is to realize that there are no absolute truths and that, in nursing as in any other discipline, our closest approximations to the truth are at best crude interpretations of very intricate and complex events. Therefore, we should always exercise a strong measure of caution when we read the exhortations of others, learning how to differentiate carefully developed arguments from hastily constructed all-embracing, difficult-to-refute statements about the world of nursing. This text attempts in some modest way to begin this process.

On discovering the nature of knowledge in a world of relationships

Len Doyal

1.1 INTRODUCTION

When I was approached to give this talk and told its title, my first response was a combination of pleasure and dismay. The pleasure derives from my respect for those in nursing who, like the organizers of this conference, really are in the vanguard of educational innovation for health profession-als. My dismay, on the other hand, concerned the vastness of the topic: 'Discovering *all* knowledge' (?) ... 'The *entire* world' (?) ... 'The *totality* of relationships' (?). However, operating with the dictum that 'anything worth doing is worth doing badly', I decided to respond by being very selective in my analysis of what I consider to be *the* key philosophical and political problem raised by the title. This is the issue of the cultural relativity of human understanding – whether or not in light of the fact that all knowledge is created against the background of specific networks of human relations and human interests, the truth and applicability of know-ledge is somehow determined by such relations and interests.

1.2 RELATIVISM AND ITS CHALLENGE

This theory of knowledge and the belief that there is nothing universal about what can be deemed rational and real is very popular. It is also, as I will argue, very dangerous. There can be no doubt, for example, that modern science and technology have been abused in the pursuit of profit. Some have maintained that such abuse is unavoidable because both types of knowledge evolved hand-in-hand with capitalism. As such, what pre-tends to be universal knowledge is seen to be irredeemably contaminated by particularity – the particularity of the social relations which gave it expression. To the degree that those social relations reflect arbitrary focal points of power and immorality, then these will be shared by the 'knowledges' they engendered.

We can see other examples of this thesis of guilt by association almost wherever we look in the intellectual and political world today. It is evident whenever someone declares that one cultural tradition cannot be criticized by another because there is no culturally neutral 'knowledge' which can be called upon to arbitrate in the matter. This is often what is going on, say, when it is argued that no moral ice is cut by whatever disgust we might find with certain cultural practices – for example female circumcision, or extreme religious persecution. Another extreme expression of such relativism is the belief that members of one culture even have the moral right to call for the death of members of another, if the call is consistent with *their* particular religious beliefs. Think of the debates surrounding those who still call for the murder of Salman Rushdie, or defend those who do? Similarly, whenever it is argued that men and women, whites and blacks, members of different social classes, members of different professions, have no interests in common and that the best that can be achieved is to live and let live, then relativism is always lurking in the background.

I will not dwell on the dangers to which I think such a conception of knowledge can lead: it seems to me that they are obvious. We live in an age when, for countless reasons, we need to search for an understanding of what binds us together as humans, wherever we live and whatever our culture. It is only in this way that we can build alliances to improve the wellbeing of everyone, and to combat those who, for whatever reason, would attempt to keep us from doing so through a process of divide and rule.

So, with this in mind, how did social relations come to be regarded as so important in determining the general scope of human knowledge? And, more important, what if anything is wrong with this view? In exploring this question, I want to tell you a little about my own intellectual development, for it has illustrated the reasons why relativism is both attractive and dangerous.

1.3 SOME PERSONAL BACKGROUND

I was born in Atlanta, Georgia, in 1944. This meant that I grew up in a culture which was just as racist, and with almost as many institutional embodiments of racism, as you will find in contemporary South Africa. It is hard to convey how taken for granted such racism can be in the socialization of a young child, especially if the culture sustains what can be termed its conceptual coherence. What I mean by this is the capacity for one part of the belief system of the culture to reinforce other parts if they come under threat, for whatever reason.

So, for example, when as a child I asked why black people were poorer, worse educated, and forced to use different public facilities from whites,

I was told that it was because they were inherently less intelligent and lacking in drive and ambition. Yet when I then pointed out that a black friend with whom I had developed a clandestine relationship could spell and do mathematics better than I could, and that his father was a lawyer whereas mine was a clerk, I was told that this must be because both he and his dad had 'white blood' – Caucasian genes – somewhere in their background. All of the whites I knew interpreted their experience of blacks in this kind of way. This is why my childhood observations of segregation led for a while to my belief that the facts confirmed the theories that legitimated racial segregation. It was a conceptually well-ordered world – if you were white; your experience of the world corresponded to what your theories told you was its reality.

For reasons which I do not completely understand to this day, from a relatively early age I began to question the truth of the racist dogma that surrounded me, despite the fact that my own observations continued to support it. I suspect that it was because psychologically it became very important to me to find fault with authority, and to begin to plan my escape from all those authorities which either rejected me, or which I myself increasingly rejected. In any case, I just began to know that somehow, something was wrong, and with that conviction I began to look for any evidence I could find that was inconsistent with the way of interpreting experience that all of my peers still accepted. Luckily, by this time we were entering the very early stages of the civil rights movement in the USA and I began hearing racism challenged on television. Then it clicked.

There *was* an alternative set of beliefs, which was easy to understand and which I could use to interpret the totality of my previous experience and explain things that I could not explain before – like the superior skills of my black friend. Generally speaking, blacks had such a hard socioeconomic time of it not because they were black, but because they were exploited. Further, whites did not realize this for two reasons: if they were also poor, it was in their psychological interest to believe that, however badly off they were, they were superior to blacks; or if they were employers, they could encourage both white and black employees to believe that their different levels of poverty were natural and unavoidable. The entire edifice of institutional racism in the South could be interpreted in this alternative way. In a sense, it was that moment of realization and what it inspired in me that led to my standing here today. Not bad for a 9-year-old who suddenly felt he had been reborn in a new world of social relations, and had been given new eyes to observe them with!

Interestingly enough, what happened to me personally was reflected in developments that were taking place at the same time in the history and philosophy of science. Until the early 1960s, the dominant theory of scientific knowledge was what in a recent book I called 'crude empiricism' (Doyal and Harris, 1986). According to this view, those in pursuit of knowledge were analogous to spectators in a position to have the truth revealed about the world or society, provided that they did nothing to distort their observational links with the realities concerned. It was argued that the aim of science should be to reason inductively, very carefully generalizing from particular facts about experience to universal theories about the world. Such theories could then be used to provide certain or very highly probable explanations of both those facts and any others like them that might be discovered. Anything that might distort the experience of these facts through the creation of bias or prejudice was viewed with anathema. The pursuit of truth was seen much as Mr. Spock of *Star Trek* sees it, as a task much more appropriate for almost any beings other than unobjective, emotional humans.

Two things happened to put paid to this bleak conception of the creation, assessment and growth of knowledge. The first was an attack on the logical and methodological foundation of empiricism. It was argued by philosophers such as Karl Popper, that certainty or even high probability in knowledge is an illusion because, given the universal claims of scientific theories, we can never prove them on the basis of our particular experience. There may always be some potential observation or experiment that might demonstrate that what we had previously believed to be true was, in fact, false. Hence it is falsification rather than verification that is the most we can hope for in science, along with the development of new theories to explain even more of the known facts than our old ones (Popper, 1972).

This kind of argument was exciting. It undermined the claims of certainty by those in authority with whom I disagreed. For even though some evidence might well confirm their beliefs – remember the example of racism – it always made sense to look for other evidence of error. The attractiveness of these ideas – that the growth of knowledge was about challenging authority, rather than accepting it – encouraged me to come to the UK to study with Popper.

Yet secondly, and approaching the mid-1960s, a more radical view of the growth of knowledge quickly caught on. This position is represented by writers such as Thomas Kuhn and Paul Feyerabend, who argued that Popper was only half right. Not only can we not prove those theories we believe to be right on the basis of observation, we cannot disprove them either – provided that we are talking about what might be termed conceptual or cultural traditions, or what Kuhn calls 'paradigms' (Kuhn, 1970; Feyerabend, 1985). Kuhn's famous example is the Copernican revolution. For someone committed to the paradigm that held that the earth is in the centre of the universe and that everything else revolves around it, the evidence is clear. Just look and you can 'see' the sun move. How could anyone who has ever witnessed a romantic Mediterranean sunset doubt it? Yet Copernicus, Kepler, Galileo and Newton came up with a different interpretation of these experiences: that what we see is a consequence of the fact of the earth's motion. Using this, they could account for the same observational experiences as the old paradigm (Kuhn, 1972).

What this shows is that you cannot pretend that facts, observations or experiments – experience in some methodological garb or other – can dictate the correctness of one conceptual tradition or the incorrectness of another. The transition from one to the other cannot be understood logically, for it is essentially irrational. The only recourse is to understand that changes in or conflicts between paradigms must, therefore, be sociological rather than logical, an explanation which primarily emphasizes those networks of social relations that reinforce some commitments and not others. For if, at the end of the day, knowledge becomes reduced to conceptual commitment, then it is social relations that determine what is rational and real. Relativism rules OK.

It is hard to convey the interest these ideas stimulated in the 1960s. As far as I was concerned, they could account for the childhood experiences I have already described. I had been converted to a new paradigm that endorsed universal civil rights, and in terms of which I then began to interpret my experiences. During the 1960s, orthodoxies seemed to be falling like houses of cards; exotic belief systems were being explored, whatever their ostensible implausibility; and ideas of tolerance seemed to dictate that it was as much the aesthetic and emotional appeal of belief systems that recommended their acceptability as it was their rationality or factuality. Indeed, so 'far out' was much of this philosophical speculation that one of the most accurate things I have heard said about the whole period is that '...if you remember the 60s, you weren't there in the first place!' Well, I remember enough of it to know that, for a while I, like so many others, was seduced by the emotional appeal of relativism. After all, what could be better, less prejudiced and, again, more tolerant than encouraging everyone to do their own thing? Isn't this why I was so opposed to racism and other forms of political and economic oppression? Two experiences, however, made me begin to think otherwise and have dominated much of my research in philosophy since. They both happened at about the same time, in the early 1970s. The first concerned a nurse at a party, whom I was desperately and aggressively trying to impress with the profundity of my beliefs about the relativity of knowledge. She said something like: 'Are you saying that you believe that all knowledge is relative to your personal perspective?' I confidently said: 'Absolutely'. She replied with one of those who-is-this-guy-smiles: 'Oh, I see ... Absolutely, relatively speaking, of course.' She then walked away with an expression of contempt that I will never forget.

The second experience was a confrontation with a moral philosopher at Oxford, to whom I also told the story of my rejection of racism as a child, and tried to articulate my strong beliefs about the existence of basic human rights. His response was much the same, though thankfully less painful than that of the nurse: 'You can't have it both ways. If you believe that racism is wrong, then it must also be wrong for those cultures which believe that it is morally right'. From the time of these experiences until today, I have tried in a number of ways to show why relativism is wrong, why the intimate link between social relations and the creation of knowledge does not entail that knowledge cannot be both universal and objective.

1.4 RELATIVISM AND THE UNIVERSALITY OF HUMAN NEED AND HUMAN RIGHTS

All I can do here is outline three key arguments to this effect. The first is that there is a range of what can be called 'technical understanding', which applies to all cultures in exactly the same way, whatever else might be specific about their systems of belief. There are some types of practical problem that all cultures have to solve successfully if they are to survive. Take agriculture, accommodation and disease as examples: food must be produced, housing must retain warmth and not fall down and, to the extent that it can be, disease must be prevented or successfully treated. To the degree that acting on some beliefs will lead to poor agricultural yields, housing that is damp rather than dry, and medicine that kills rather than prevents or cures, it will be irrational to act on them.

Technical understanding which is successful in all of these respects will be so irrespective of the social relations that characterize the specific culture in which it is used. This is why, for example, access to appropriate antibiotic care is desired by everyone who understands its practical effectiveness, whatever their other cultural beliefs about medicine, health and illness. Generally speaking, therefore, successful technical understanding – natural science and technology at their best – enables us to intervene in the world with predictable results. Human relations are irrelevant to such success, although certainly relevant to its abuse (Doyal and Harris, 1986).

So, what would it mean for relativists to claim that such knowledge was only relevant to the particular culture that generated it? Suppose they possessed the appropriate antibiotics and were confronted by someone suffering from bacterial pneumonia in a culture practising non-western medicine. Would they not advocate their use? Who knows or cares in what kind of patriarchal and hierarchical culture an invention as useful as the wheel was discovered? Are not the harmful effects of modern weapons the same for both fundamentalist Christians and Muslims?

The second type of knowledge I believe exists concerns human needs. There are good arguments to show that the degree to which individuals achieve their physical, intellectual and emotional potential will be dependent on the scope and success of their participation in the social life that surrounds them (Doyal and Gough, 1991). Successful participation will be impossible, and individuals will be seriously harmed in the process, unless they somehow manage to achieve two specific goals, which are the same for everyone whatever their cultural background. It is these goals –

which must be achieved in order to achieve any other goals – that I call basic human needs. The first such need is the absence of serious physical disease and the accompanying experience of illness. You can hardly participate in your culture to the full if you are disabled for biomedical reasons which are perfectly well understood. Individual autonomy is the second universal human need: this is both the intellectual competence to formulate aims and beliefs in the context of one's social environment, and to possess the emotional confidence to be able to act accordingly in sustained and consistent ways.

Of course, we must differentiate between such universal needs and those things required to satisfy specific cultures – certain types of food or educational training, for example. However, provided that we adhere to this distinction, it should be clear that the basic need for health and autonomy is the same for everyone, whatever their culture. It should be equally clear that we have a great deal of knowledge about how both types of goals must be achieved. Indeed, it is empirical data based on this knowledge that organizations such as the World Health Organisation and the World Bank employ in their international evaluations of economic and social progress.

Third, I think we can show that all humans have the same rights: the right to an optimal level of basic need satisfaction. The argument is quite simple: we all believe that we and others have moral duties of various kinds, even if we disagree about what exactly they are. If you really believe in the correctness of any moral code – whatever its cultural underpinnings – it must follow that you believe that everyone has a duty to be good on your terms. If you do not, then your conception of the good would not be that good after all, would it? For example, if murder or the rejection of a particular religious creed is really believed to be morally wrong for one person, it must follow that it should be regarded as morally wrong for everyone, even if this is not in fact the case. This means that you must at least believe that people should have the right to do what *you* think right to the best of their ability. However, for them to be able to do so, it follows from the preceding argument that their basic needs must be satisfied to high and not just minimum levels. Consistency, therefore, along with your own conviction about your vision of the good commits you to believing in the right of everyone to have what is necessary for them to participate optimally in the same vision. Again, if you did not wish this, then how could your beliefs about the good be that good? This will be so whatever the particular content of your moral code. The fact that so many people do not respect this right is more an indication of their own irrationality than a confirmation of the thesis of the cultural relativity of moral understanding.

In general, then, if we are going to believe in the possibility of human progress and liberation, we have to have some way to measure how we are doing. Try telling my childhood black friend – who, by the way, is now a highly successful lawyer – that racial progress has not been made since he and I were children, and he will laugh in your face. The fact that there is still so much room for improvement on this score only further underlines the fact that we do have measures which we believe we can use to evaluate progress in combating racism, wherever it exists. My point is simple: if we can use such technological, intellectual and moral standards to criticize one culture – that of racism – then to be consistent we must believe that all cultures should be evaluated in the same terms. And whenever we evaluate progress in this way, we also reject relativism in the process.

Finally, what does all of this have to do with nursing and being a 'good' nurse? There are two basic principles of ethics for both nursing and medicine which are explicit or implicit in all of the professional codes of good moral conduct. The first is the universal duty of good clinical care – to use your expertise to protect the life and health of your patient to an acceptable standard. The second is the universal duty to respect the autonomy of your patient – their right to informed consent, their right to correct information about their illness and treatment (and enough of it to make informed consent a practical proposition) and their right to confidentiality. In one way or another, both of these principles are always explicit or implicit in debates about what constitutes good moral medicine, but what is the origin of the rights of patients and duties of nurses as underlined by both principles? Given the justifiable emphasis in nursing on the importance of feeling in properly caring for patients, does the answer to this question also call upon emotion? Certainly, if this were all there were to it, we would be thrown back into precisely the relativism that I have tried to argue that we must avoid. For the fact is, that in the same clinical situation, the feelings of nurses often dictate different and conflicting actions. This is why we need an explanation of the origin of these principles which calls upon reason rather than feeling. The theory of needs outlined above provides just such understanding (Doyal, 1992).

No doubt you will believe that both you and your patients have certain duties as good citizens from the perspective of your own moral commitments, whatever they are. Having chosen to have medical treatment, one of the patient's duties might be to act responsibly to get better through rigidly following whatever plan of medical management has been prescribed. Yet for such beliefs about the duties of patients to be consistent, i.e. for this to be a practical proposition, you must also believe that they possess the basic needs of health and autonomy and that you have a duty to help to provide access to the clinical conditions for their optimal satisfaction. You must do your best, in short, to protect their life and health and to respect their autonomy – exactly the explanation we were looking for! Otherwise, again, your patients will not be in a position to do their best to be both good patients and good citizens in *your* moral terms.

1.5 CONCLUSION

What I have tried (all too briefly) to do here is to make it clear that some beliefs about moral duties are not based on emotion or simply the preference of one from many cultural traditions. Rather, they follow from rational argument, of the sort which is our only hope in ordering our personal and international affairs in ways that do not arbitrarily harm others, including the patients for whom we are professionally responsible.

What is at stake in not recognizing this, is the relativizing of human suffering for the sake of the false emotional comfort of thinking that we are being tolerant. So, returning to the theme of this paper, universal knowledge in the face of differing human relations does exist, and we have a lot of it. To deny this on the grounds of cultural relativity is both morally wrong and politically dangerous.

POINTS FOR DISCUSSION

Nicky James chaired the session and began by suggesting that, rather than being an easy option, actually coping with relativism creates personal, professional and political tensions, because people have to act. Action was the consequence of committing oneself to principles; having to make judgements and having a sense of priority were the inevitable consequences of taking a position, whether one of universalism or one of relativism. She began the debate by offering an example and asked what we would do if we were faced with a white person at the end of their life who refused to be cared for by a black nurse. Would we accept their right to such a preference or would it be giving in to another person's prejudice? Is relativism dangerous? Where do we allow for weakness? Do basic human needs exist and are they the same for everyone? And if they are the same, what political agendas do they throw up?

Following these opening remarks, the first set of comments centred around the issue of respecting patients' right to information about their condition, and linked to this the point that professionals could neither play scientific nor moral God. This notion linked with the underlying question of how could another person, whether it be a professional or not, make a judgement about what another person – a patient – should think or do. Linked with this discussion was a question about the danger of universal principles leading to dictatorship of certain ideologies: it is important to distinguish those things in culture which are acceptably diversified and those which are not. Several illustrations were offered from everyday practice which indicated that rather than being an academic point, the difference between what one would expect to be universally acceptable and what one would not, was often open to debate, for example, truth telling, individual autonomy (especially for women) and justice.

The relationship between technical and moral knowledge within a particular culture was readdressed during the discussion time. What happens in situations where belief goes against pragmatics? For example, the child of Jehovah's Witness parents is given a blood transfusion against the parents' wishes because the professionals believe they have a responsibility to save the child's life: are we in danger of violating patients' values on the ground that they do not conform to universal truths? What are the consequences of such actions? This particular case provoked much discussion, with numerous considerations of what was the most correct thing to do. The perspective taken by the group was very much linked with the effect such actions would have on the future relationship between the child and its parents. This was interesting, as the decision to save the child was being made almost on speculations as to whether or not they would be rejected by the parents.

The discussion moved on to consider the role of authority in arriving at universal principles. The debate went back to an earlier point, which was: how can you ensure that so-called universal truths are not just one particular group's view of the world being imposed on everyone else? This question was essentially one of the central themes of Doyal's paper, and it was the recourse to reflecting on what most people cherished and valued that enabled one to obtain a sense of universals. In a similar vein, the question was asked about how groups who start off at different points come to understand and communicate with one another.

REFERENCES

Doyal, L. (1992) Needs, rights and the moral duties of clinicians, in *Principles of Health Care*, (ed. R. Gillon) Wiley, Chichester.

Doyal, L. and Gough, I. (1991) *A Theory of Human Need*, Macmillan, London.

Doyal, L. and Harris, R. (1986) *Empiricism, Explanation and Rationality*, Routledge, London.

Feyerabend, P. (1985) Collected Papers: Vol. 1, *Realism, Rationalism and Scientific Method*, Cambridge University Press, Cambridge.

Kuhn, T. (1970) *The Structure of Scientific Revolutions*, Chicago University Press, Chicago.

Kuhn, T. (1972) *The Copernican Revolution*, Harvard University Press, Cambridge, Mass.

Popper, K. (1972) *Conjectures and Refutations*, Routledge, London.

The ideological foundations of informal care

Gillian Dalley

2.1 INTRODUCTION

This paper looks at some of the issues surrounding the process of caring for sick and dependent people in society; in particular it considers the development of a particular policy – namely, that of community care – which relies on the provision of a mix of formal and informal care. It argues that there are a number of ideological associations involved in different forms of caring, in particular drawing attention to a contrast between individualism and collectivism. It suggests that the consequences for women and for dependent people are largely determined by these ideological foundations.

2.2 THE DEVELOPMENT OF COMMUNITY CARE

Community care as a key government policy objective began in 1962, when Enoch Powell, as Health Minister, announced radical plans for a 15-year programme of hospital-bed closures, with the expectation that psychiatric patients would in the future be cared for outside hospitals, 'in the community'. Ideas about caring for people outside hospital, however, had begun some years earlier, when new methods of treating psychiatric patients – in association with new drug therapies – were introduced. It had gradually become acceptable to think that mentally ill people did not have to be locked away in seclusion from the rest of society (Jones, 1972).

During the 1970s, more general views about community care began to develop. What had first begun as a new way of treating psychiatric patients came to be seen as being applicable to other client groups. A white paper, *Better services for the mentally handicapped* (DHSS, 1971) was published, advocating care in the community for all mentally handicapped people; the closure of the long-stay hospitals which had characterized the management of mental handicap for more than 100 years became a long-term goal. A parallel white paper (DHSS, 1975) setting out similar objectives for the care of mentally ill people was published a few years later. At the same time, academics and pressure groups were thinking seriously about how future policies should look. Bayley (1973), for example, looked at the role family and community were playing in caring for people outside hospitals. He made the distinction between care *in* the community and care *by* the community, stressing that there was an important conceptual distinction between them and that care *by* the community was perhaps the more significant.

The Labour government published a major policy document in the mid-1970s (DHSS, 1976) which mapped out future developments. It marked the first attempt to devise a national strategy to rank particular patient groups in order of priority, and also to ensure an equitable distribution of resources. In doing so, it sought to give precedence to the 'Cinderella' groups – defined as elderly, mentally ill, mentally handicapped and physically handicapped people – over other patient groups. Other policy documents followed, backing up the strategy of trying to shift resources towards these priority groups, at the same time linking it to a commitment to community care.

Community care as a component of government policy was seen initially as the process of cutting down institutional provision, partly as a cost-saving device, and replacing it with small-scale residential provision and domiciliary services. Little mention was made of the role of informal care, apart from the recognition that many people were maintained in their own homes. With the change of government in 1979, greater emphasis began to be placed on the moral responsibility of families to care for their relatives. *Growing Older* (DHSS, 1981), for example, stressed the importance of family care, stating that the professional services were of secondary importance.

While it is clear that the introduction of community care was prompted by developments in the medical management of patients and the consequent decision to reduce the number of long-stay hospital beds, there were other reasons why community care became the preferred policy option during the 1970s. One was the hope that it would be a cheaper form of care; another was the growing recognition of the demographic changes which were being forecast for the 1990s and beyond, and their implications. It was gradually coming to be realized that the numbers of very elderly people were going to grow at a substantial rate over the following 20 years and that institutional provision would be unable to cope with the increase. It was projected, for example, that there would be an 80% increase in the number of people aged over 85 between 1971 and 2001, representing a total of 348 000 people (OPCS, 1978). At the same time, there would be a proportionately lower number of younger people in the labour force able to fill the jobs in the traditional caring institutions – hospitals, nursing and residential homes. In addition, the numbers of younger physically and mentally handicapped people were likely to survive longer than in the past, placing further demands on the caring services (Illsley, 1981).

The problem of how the health and social services were likely to be able to cope with these increases gradually became apparent during the course of the 1970s, and was clearly one of the stimuli leading to the policy that called for a major shift in resources towards the priority groups. And, as more attention was given to the care needs of these groups, greater attention gradually came to be focused on those who provided some of the care for them. Although initially it was assumed that community care would be less costly than institutional care, and was thus an attractive policy option, it was gradually recognized that this was unlikely to be the case. Perhaps this has been one of the reasons why informal family care has come to be seen as such an important part of community care provision. The document on old age published by the Conservative government in 1981, *Growing Older*, stated:

'The primary sources of support and care for elderly people are informal and voluntary. These spring from the personal ties of kinship, friendship and neighbourhood... . Care in the community must increasingly mean care *by* the community.'

Worries about the costs of formal care provision and the growth in numbers of those requiring care were clearly important factors in focusing on the importance of informal care, but informal care also fitted the philosophy of self-reliant individualism and anti-statism which characterized the Thatcher government throughout the 1980s. According to this philosophy, responsibility for the care of the individual should lie first with the individual him/herself and then with his/her family. The state should play a subsidiary role in what should essentially be a private arrangement among kin. As in other areas of human activity, the state – according to this view – should withdraw as far as possible.

Ironically, as more and more emphasis was placed on the role of informal care, the very act of drawing attention to it revealed many of the difficulties associated with it. Whereas during the 1970s very little was heard about the part played by kin in caring for dependent people, the 1980s saw a mushrooming of concern for them. A new term – carers – became commonplace, and interest began to grow in who and how numerous they were. The first interest was expressed by feminists, who argued that community care was another way of labelling what was essentially care by female relatives. Finch and Groves (1980) wrote a paper arguing that community care policies threatened women's rights to equality of opportunity in social and economic life. The Equal Opportunities Commission (1982) published a research report 2 years later taking up these issues and reviewing the available evidence about the extent and character of informal caring, especially by women. A campaign developed end eligibility for the Invalid Care Allowance (introduced in 1975) arried women (eventually successful in 1986) as a means of recogniz- the role played by women in informal care.

Gradually, carers came to be recognized as a legitimate interest group. The Association of Carers was set up in 1982, later merging with the National Council for Carers and their Elderly Dependants to form the Carers' National Association, to represent the interests of carers. The DHSS funded the establishment of a carers' support unit at the King's Fund in 1985. Although carers' needs were not initially recognized under the social security reforms of the mid-1980s, in spite of active campaigning on their behalf, a carer's premium under the Income Support scheme has been introduced from April 1991. And in the most recent White Papers preceding the *NHS and Community Care Act, 1990* the interests of carers were specifically emphasized. Out of all this, there has been a growing recognition that the cost of informal caring is not cheap; but it is a cost that is often born by the carer her/himself rather than by the state, unlike the formal services provided either through the health service or the personal social services.

Along with this recognition has gone a parallel understanding that the formal services themselves are failing to fulfil the role expected of them – even the role designated for them in the 'hands off' political climate of the 1980s. A number of reports throughout the decade have drawn attention to failures in provision. The Social Services Select Committee in 1985 pointed to gaps in the services for mentally ill people being discharged into the community (House of Commons, 1985). The Audit Commission in 1986 produced a comprehensive critique of community care services which prompted the government to commission Sir Roy Griffiths to look into the subject and make recommendations for future policy. His report (Griffiths, 1988) drew attention to major failures in collaboration between the health and social services (seen as the key to effective provision), muddled boundaries of responsibility, and a lack of urgency in dealing with problems. He recommended that local authorities be given lead responsibility for community care and that resources allocated to that sector be rigidly protected ('ring-fenced'). The government took up many of his recommendations in the White Paper *Caring for People* (DH, 1989), which later formed part of the 1990 Act. However, the implementation of many of the key provisions in the Act has been delayed because of cost implications. Community care policy, therefore, is in some disarray.

2.3 THE PROCESS OF CARING

Defining what is meant by caring is complex. There are professional definitions: for example, medical care differs from nursing care; continuous nursing care differs from continuous care. Upon such definitions may depend policies for employment and recruitment. Current debate about what constitutes the nursing task revolves in some measure around definitions; the boundaries between skilled care which can only be performed by qualified nurses, and other forms of care which may be undertaken by a variety of support or auxiliary staff, are open to negotiation. Further, there are parallel definitions. The distinction which Griffiths (1988) made between health and social care has been built into government policy in the White Paper *Caring for People*, and subsequent legislation, for example, is based on the boundaries between agencies rather than professions. In practice, the distinction is proving to be untenable; the tasks that one professional group performs cannot always be dissected and separated into their constituent health or social care elements and thus reallocated across agency boundaries.

There is a further distinction – that between formal and informal care, which is the focus of this paper. Broadly speaking, the distinction centres on the contrast between paid and unpaid work. Formal care is that which is provided by paid workers employed either by the statutory agencies (the health service or local authorities), by the private sector or by voluntary organizations. Informal care is more complex: it may be provided by kin – in particular, close kin such as parents, spouses, sons and daughters – or by friends and neighbours or even volunteers from local organizations; it may be provided regularly and intensively, or intermittently and lightly; it generally encompasses what Griffiths would classify as social care, although it also includes tasks which nurses generally perform: for example, lifting, washing, the administering of some medication and changing dressings. Other tasks performed may be less intensive, including shopping, cleaning, laundry, companionship and financial management.

The extent to which any of these forms of caring is provided depends on a number of unpredictable factors. First, it depends on the domestic circumstances of the dependent person. Does he or she live alone or with other kin? Has he or she always lived under these arrangements? The presence of kin who are familiar with the dependent person may mean there is a greater likelihood of her/him being cared for informally. Secondly, the range of formal services available in a particular locality is also likely to have a bearing: where there are few services, the greater is the likelihood that the dependent person will have to rely on informal care (however appropriate). A third factor may be cost, as formal services are becoming increasingly costly and may be beyond the means of many dependent people and their kin. A fourth factor may be the views of those requiring care: some people may have strong preferences about the sort of care they would like. Whether their wishes can be satisfied is rarely guaranteed, and depends on a mix of the three factors outlined above.

What does this mean in practice? We know from the 1985 *General Household Survey* (Green, 1988) that there are over 6 million people who classify themselves as carers of one degree or another. In addition, we know something about the extent of formal services available – residential care, day care, respite care, domiciliary care (Qureshi, 1991). We also know that there is a general view that these services are insufficient and are likely to remain so (indeed, to become scarcer). As mentioned earlier, government policy has been predicated on an assumption that the bulk of care will be provided by families.

If we examine what this means in practical terms, it becomes clear that the role of informal care will become increasingly important as the number of very elderly people grows and the number of mentally ill people discharged from institutions or failing to find any form of formal care swells. None of the policy documents fully acknowledges the nature of the burden that will be placed on informal carers. They recognize that carers have a need for information about support services, and that their interests should be taken into account (along with the interests of those they are caring for) when decisions about formal care are being made, but they do not go into the detail of what informal care in many instances actually means in practice.

Informal care differs from formal care not only because of the absence of payment, but also because of the nature of the relationships established between those caring and those cared for. Existing relationships of love, affection, obligation or hostility are overlaid by the overwhelming duties of caring. Family members often feel they have no choice about whether to care or not, even though it may mean considerable sacrifice. But feelings are often contradictory: people may want to care, regarding it as an expression of undoubted love for their relatives, and yet at the same time not want to give up their other social activities and responsibilities. Thus they may feel resentful and find it difficult to reconcile these mixed feelings, especially when burdened by the exacting duties of caring that they have to perform, often without any extra support. In other cases, people may find they have to care for relatives for whom they have little affection, bound into the caring relationship through a sense of guilt and duty or simply through circumstance. Again, coping with such feelings while performing the caring tasks may be hard to bear.

2.4 IDEOLOGICAL UNDERCURRENTS

These, then, are some of the practical difficulties involved in the process of caring. There are other, less explicit, issues, namely those which are ideological and which raise serious questions about the nature of current community care policies. They cover a number of fields: gender relations, the politics of disability, the appropriate role of the state and the place of institutional care.

2.4.1 Gender relations

A distinction is often made between the process of 'caring about' and 'caring for' (Parker, 1981; Graham, 1983) and it is sometimes linked to the difference in involvement of men and women in the caring process.

According to this distinction, 'caring about' is an affective process, to do with the displaying of concern for others, while 'caring for' represents the practical tasks of tending for someone who is dependent. The present writer has argued elsewhere (Dalley, 1988) that the two processes are most commonly perceived as joined together in the role of motherhood. Thus the two become indissolubly associated as a fundamental part of women's social role, which is thence applied to other areas of life – notably to caring *for* other relatives (besides young children) *about* whom they also care.

Men's roles are not defined in this way. Men may care *about* their family and friends but less often *for* them. Society's expectation of them, rather, is that they should be 'responsible for' – perhaps in financial terms, the traditional 'paterfamilias' role. Although it has been argued that the statistics show that there are many men who are carers (Green, 1988), a majority of these are pensioners caring for their spouses (Arber and Ginn, 1991); the responsibilities that elderly spouses have for each other may be rather different from the responsibilities that younger men and women have for their kin in general. Responsibility for mutual caring seems to be part of the 'normal' contractual relationship of marriage; most elderly people would perhaps accept that caring for each other in old age was an expected and acceptable obligation, in the same way that parents care for and about their children.

The division between the roles of women and men in relation to caring is a reflection of a more fundamental division. Again, the writer has argued that this division forms the basis for an ideology of 'familism' which underlies and validates the present formation of our society:

'A view that holds women to be caring to the point of self-sacrifice is propagated at all levels of thought and action; it figures in art and literature, it is the prop of official social welfare policies, and it is the currency in which the social exchanges within marriage and the domestic sphere are transacted. It means that women accept the validity of this view as readily as men do. And once this central tenet – of women's natural propensity to care (in contradistinction to men's nature – is accepted, the locus for caring then becomes determined. With woman as carer, man becomes provider; the foundation of the nuclear family is laid. It becomes the ideal model to which all should approximate.' (Dalley, 1988).

Moreover, this pattern of gender roles becomes the ideal model for caring – the 'family model of care'. According to this model, care is best provided in a family setting, at home, wherever possible by a family member (usually expected to be the woman). Rosy pictures are conjured up of the warmth of family life, set against a backdrop of a close-knit, supportive community. It becomes enshrined in official discourse:

'When help is needed families are, as they have always been, the principal source of support and care. They are usually best placed to understand and meet the wide variety of personal needs which arise and their support is irreplaceable. It may often involve considerable personal sacrifice, particularly where the "family" is one person, often a single woman, caring for an elderly relative.' (*Growing Older*)

and

'Families, friends, neighbours and other local people provide the majority of care in response to needs which they are uniquely well placed to identify and respond to... . The first task of publicly provided services is to support and where possible strengthen these networks of carers.' (Griffiths, 1988)

Where such family care is not available, 'surrogate family care' becomes the favoured model. Institutional care is closed down and residents are moved into small-scale 'family-like' group homes and hostels; children are fostered in families rather than cared for in children's homes; 'granny fostering' has been encouraged by a number of social services departments. There is a strong consensus among policy-makers and practitioners that such forms of care are the preferred option, and contrary views are regarded as heretical, although institutions are being closed with little evaluation of their alternatives being undertaken and fostering arrangements have a disturbingly high rate of breakdown. Old people are maintained at home entirely alone, with a perplexing mixture of services perhaps being brought in, but often with very little support, on the pretext that home-based care is what old people want.

The enormous growth in the private residential care sector during the 1990s is regretted by policy-makers and practitioners precisely because it represents a rejection of this home-based model of care which they have favoured. Much of the recent community care legislation was introduced specifically to curb this growth.

Community care, then, is based on an ideology of familism which in turn rests on a gendered division of labour within the domestic sphere. This extends beyond expected areas of responsibility into the sphere of caring, and has the effect of binding women into caring relationships whether they wish it or not. Furthermore, beyond the family context, the model has an ideological force which determines forms of care in other contexts too.

2.4.2 The politics of disability

This family model of care rests on the expectation of women's altruism, or what Land and Rose have called compulsory altruism (Land and Rose, 1985). The reverse side of the coin of altruism is the passive receipt of that altruism. People who are the dependants in the caring relationship have little choice but to accept the care that is given; there are few alternatives. Thus both sides are bound together, however reluctantly, by ties of duty, gratitude, sacrifice and dependency. And yet if we listen to what disabled people say about the issue of care and the sort of service they look for, it is precisely the powerlessness of the dependant's role that they reject (Oliver, 1990). They resist roles that are ascribed to them – to be grateful for help received, to be patient in the face of rejection, to be passive. In terms of the sort of service they would prefer, they look for those which will promote their independence. Thus they argue against institutions because they inhibit their freedom: they see them as prisons. But the alternative is not necessarily in the direction of forms of care and services based on the family model of care. The straitjacket of dependency on the altruism of close kin or the isolation of living alone with minimal community care support may be as oppressive as the old forms of institutional care.

Nevertheless, the onward march towards community care proceeds (although shortage of resources may hold it up from time to time). Under the new legislation, disabled people will have their care needs assessed by professional assessors (who may also be budget holders); such assessors are charged to take the interests of carers and those for whom they care into account. It takes place within a framework that denies the validity of any form of care other than the home-based family model. Residential, nursing home or hospital care are regarded as (expensive) last resorts. Alternative forms of care are rarely encouraged; there is no recognition of active participation in forms of self help, for example, or communities of independent living. Further, it does not place the power of choice in the hands of disabled people themselves. It simply confirms the model of dependent people as dependent, and carers as carers. It represents an ideology of compulsory altruism, passivity and individualism.

2.4.3 The appropriate role of the state

With the emphasis placed on the family model of care, the role of the professional services and of the state come into question. During the past decade, state provision of services has come under attack. An ideology of sturdy self-reliance and possessive individualism which can be traced back to the growth of capitalism 200 years ago has been fostered (Dalley, 1988). In spite of four decades of the welfare state, policy now is based quite clearly on the proposition that the state should play a reduced role in the provision of social welfare: at most, it becomes the enabler and regulator. Those who espouse the individualist cause place emphasis on individual liberty, competition and the market, arguing that this will best serve people's interests; the poor and the sick will benefit from the 'tenderness' which tempers the competitiveness and materialism of the individualist (Joseph and Sumption, 1979).

However, there is an alternative ideology – one which fuelled much of the movement towards the policies upon which the welfare state was founded, namely, that of collectivism. Collectivists argue that without mutual support and the fostering of social responsibility through collective organization, the weakest in society will lose out. Contrary to the assertions of individualists that the market and, failing that, the tenderness of particular individuals, will solve all problems, collectivists believe that under market conditions the poor and the sick will be thrown into unwilling dependency on the selective goodwill of other people. Thus the charitable 'do-gooding' concern of the free and the powerful becomes the only salvation for the dependent and powerless. Collectivism, in contrast, stresses the importance of a social order based on the values of reciprocity, fellowship and cooperation. Social responsibility for the poor and the weak, vested in state and community organizations, becomes the concern of all and does not become dependent on the whim of the powerful and successful. It is thus possible to ensure dignity and autonomy to all members of society.

According to this view, it is both moral and efficacious for the state – the collectivity – to provide services for its more dependent members. There is a further logic: if it is right for the state to take responsibility, then it is wrong for it to abdicate it and require the family (that is, women) to take it up *unless* they have actively chosen to do so (free of any sense of obligation or pressure). Thus policies that are predicated on the assumption and requirement that informal care – that is, care which does not emanate from the collective responsibility of the state – should and will provide the core of provision, are clear rejections of the collectivist philosophy.

2.5 ALTERNATIVES TO INFORMAL CARE

If informal care is unacceptable first because it imposes too great a burden on women and, very often, on the people they care for, and second, because it represents the abdication of collective responsibility, it is necessary to look for alternatives. Institutional care, in all its forms, is widely regarded as unacceptable, largely because of the poor reputation many of the long-stay psychiatric hospitals have acquired over the years. No-one would recommend a return to that form of provision (although it is worth noting that such institutions represented a very large investment of resources in the care of mental illness by Victorian society which has not been matched since). Nevertheless , if the isolation and fragmentation of community care on the one hand, and the warehousing of the large institutions on the other, is to be avoided, it may be worth looking with greater approval at other forms of collective or group care.

Communities based on independent living principles, retirement villages where elderly people take responsibility for each other within a framework of support services, neighbourhood provision of day care for young children, are all examples of the way forward. Lessons can be learnt from abroad, from Scandinavia and from the United States. Lessons can also be learnt closer to home. Increasing numbers of elderly people from Britain take holidays abroad, living together in hotels for the winter season; there is no stigma attached to this as there is with some forms of residential care provided in Britain. Even the notion of 'stigma' may be questioned: some have argued that the large increase in the numbers of old people going into nursing homes during the past decade – made possible inadvertently by changes in social security regulations – is the biggest demonstration of the exercise of freedom of choice by elderly working class people that has ever been known (Halsey, 1990). It is reminiscent of Aneurin Bevan's hope that old people's homes to be provided under the 1948 National Assistance Act would allow such freedom: 'any old people who wish to go may go there in exactly the same way as many well-to-do people have been accustomed to go into residential hotels' (Means and Smith, 1983). The *Daily Mail* at the time suggested that these homes should be called 'sunshine hotels'.

It is possible, therefore, to devise forms of care and support that do not rely overwhelmingly on the informal care of family and friends. It requires thought and imagination to ensure that the mistakes of the past are not repeated; however, there are enough examples to demonstrate that this may be forthcoming.

2.6 CONCLUSION

This paper has focused on community care, a major component of current policy for the care of dependent people, and examined the ideological foundations of individualism on which it is based. It argues that there are a number of consequences which stem from this configuration. Heavy burdens are placed on families – mostly women; sick, disabled and infirm people have little freedom of choice and are locked into relationships of dependency or left alone in isolation. The responsibility tends to fall on women because women's position is determined by the same ideological forces which underlie current social welfare policies. Those who are cared for are forced into relationships of dependency because they are powerless and have no freedom of action.

The paper also suggests that there is a contrary approach, namely that based on collectivism. Collectivism is the ideological opposite of individualism; it underlies those policies in the past which have fostered broad social responsibility for all members of society, especially the poor and the weak, without relying on the compulsory altruism of one section of the population on the one hand, or the selectively charitable instincts of the powerful, wealthy few on the other.

Lastly, some alternatives have been mooted, albeit briefly. Many of the existing alternatives to community care and the reliance on informal care within it, are either unacceptable or heavily stigmatized. The argument in this paper is that there are alternatives that collectivist approaches can produce which do not require the compulsory altruism of women and do not force disabled and infirm people into unacceptable relationships of dependency.

POINTS FOR DISCUSSION

Dalley's paper takes the debate about caring – and the professional's responsibility in providing such a service – one step closer to everyday reality. In the previous paper, Doyal argued that there should be a set of universally recognized principles to which individuals in whatever society can be expected to adhere. Such principles relate to the right of every individual to benefit from the advances of technology, the right to a quality of life which is disease free, and has a right to exercise his authority in terms of his own rights and obligations.

In her paper, Dalley explores how the notion of caring for ill and dependent people has been interpreted from a policy point of view. Using community care policy as the vehicle, Dalley argues that, rather than recognizing the needs or wishes of individuals requiring care and equally taking note of the needs of those informal carers expected to provide it, government policy in past decades has been about setting up a system which discriminates against the client and their unpaid (usually female) carer. This approach, Dalley argues, has suited government policy makers, politicians and professionals alike. Her view is that the whole policy of community care is forwarded on a number of false premises, and these should be changed to better reflect the desires and wishes of clients and carers.

The main themes to emerge from the discussion following the paper were considerations of the changing role of the professional care giver, issues surrounding the funding of community care in the light of the emergence of contracts, and the possibility of the introduction of a voucher system. A third area to be explored was the way in which professional groups labelled their values or beliefs regarding community care, and a final area explored looked at the myth or reality of policies such as community care.

During the discussion a number of questioners came back to explore the theme of the changing role of the professional. Specifically, a central area was whether the professional – in this case the district nurse or health visitor – operated as an agent of social control. If direct care was moving from the hands of paid professionals to unpaid relatives and friends, then was the professional's role one of checking to see if these unpaid workers were doing the job to an acceptable level? This was an unattractive idea but did have some authenticity, given the changes that were taking place in the working experiences of nurses. More acceptable roles for professional care givers were discussed, and these were described in terms of the professional being a partner or cooperator in care alongside the unpaid carer, or equally being an activist, helping the client and carers to obtain the sort of support they needed.

Linked to the growing ambiguous role of the professional care giver was the problem of the professional being the budget-holder for the service. Thus, a common scenario could emerge that certain benefits would not be offered to clients and their carers because the professional was trying to keep within budget. The moral dilemma this poses for professionals was acknowledged but no satisfactory solutions were given. One approach, however, was to be found in providing the client with more choice through the new purchasing – providing mechanism being set up in health units. If clients knew that they could choose between services, they would be able to demand services more in line with their requirements. The question of whether a voucher system would be introduced for clients was discussed. Similar to the proposed school voucher system, it was agreed that if clients and their carers could buy the sort of service they wanted, this would protect both parties against the implicit paternalism of professional groups. However, a number of factors militated against any real uptake for community care vouchers, the central factor being the unpredictable nature of the severity and extent of the need, and hence the difficulty in allocating for it.

The reality of professional team-work was brought into question when discussing how effective health and social services were in identifying and meeting clients' needs. There was widespread agreement that effective team-work was more of a myth than a reality. Reasons being given for this included the way that professionals were trained to think in terms of individual cases, e.g. *my patient*, rather than having collective responsibility both for individual patients and for groups of patients. The problem of arbitrary professional boundaries had still not been solved and the advent of budgeting for services was making the service even more fragmented on a task-based approach.

The final area to be explored looked at how relevant particular policies can be to those who have to carry them out. The supreme irony of the community care policy was that managers up and down the country believed that it happened, and indeed were setting objectives for it, but the reality was that nothing really was happening. People were being cared for by unpaid relatives and friends and a small minority were being provided with paid professional services. The only way out of this impasse, according to Dalley, was to empower local groups to demand a better service from the professionals, and more importantly, to expect the collective community to provide that wide range of services needed to care for frail, elderly, dependent people. It was as much a question of dispelling the myth of family life and the sacrifice of the female in providing unpaid care, as it was of awakening the whole community to its responsibility to care for its more dependent members. This was a message accepted and shared by the mainly nursing audience.

REFERENCES

Arber, S. and Ginn, J. (1990) The meaning of informal care: gender and the contribution of elderly people. *Ageing and Society*, **10**, 4.

Audit Commission (1986) *Making a Reality of Community Care*, Audit Commission, London.

Bayley, M. (1973) *Mental Handicap and Community Care*, Routledge and Kegan Paul, London.

Dalley, G. (1988) *Ideologies of Caring; Rethinking Community and Collectivism*, Macmillan, London.

Department of Health (1989) *Caring for people*, (White Paper), HMSO, London.

DHSS (1971) *Better Services for the Mentally Handicapped*, Cmnd 4683, HMSO, London.

DHSS (1975) *Better Services for the Mentally Ill*, Cmnd. 6233, HMSO, London.

DHSS (1976) *Priorities for Health and Personal Social Services in England*, HMSO, London.

DHSS (1981) *Growing Older*, Cmnd 8173, HMSO, London.

Equal Opportunities Commission (1982) *Caring for the Elderly and Handicapped: Community Care Policies and Women's Lives*, EOC, Manchester.

Finch, J. and Groves, D. (1980) Community care and the family: a case for equal opportunities. *Journal of Social Policy*, **9**, 4

Graham, H. (1983) Caring: a labour of love, in *Labour of Love: Women, Work and Caring*, (eds J. Finch and D. Groves), Routledge and Kegan Paul, London.

Green, H. (1988) *Informal Carers (General Household Survey/OPCS)*, HMSO, London.

Griffiths, R. (1988) *Community Care: Agenda for Action*, HMSO, London.

Halsey, A. H. (1990) Radio 4 programme, December.

House of Commons (1985) *Community Care with Special Reference to Adult Mentally Ill and Mentally Handicapped People*. Second report from the Social Services Select Committee, Session 1984–85, HMSO, London.

Illsley, R. (1981) Problems of dependency groups: the care of the elderly, the handicapped and the chronically ill. *Social Science and Medicine*, **15A**,

Jones, K. (1972) *A History of the Mental Health Services*, Routledge and Kegan Paul, London.

Joseph, K. and Sumption, J. (1979) *Equality*, John Murray, London.

Land, H. and Rose, H. (1985) Compulsory altruism for some or an altruistic society for all? in *In Defence of Welfare*, (eds, P. Bean, J. Ferris, and D. Whynes), Tavistock Publications, London.

Means, R. and Smith, R. (1983) From public assistance institutions to 'sunshine' hotels: changing state perceptions about residential care for the elderly, in *Ageing in Modern Society*, (ed D. Jerrome), Croom Helm, London.

Oliver, M. (1990) *The Politics of Disablement*, Macmillan, London.

OPCS (1978) *Population trends No. 22*, OPCS, London.

Parker, R. (1981) Tending and social policy, in *A New Look at the Social Services*, (eds E. M. Goldberg, and S. Hatch), Discussion paper 4, Policy Studies Institute, London.

Qureshi, H. (1991) Services for disabled people, in *Disability and Social Policy*, (ed. G. Dalley), Policy Studies Institute, London.

3

Formalizing concepts related to nursing and caring

Alison Kitson

3.1 INTRODUCTION

I would like to start off my excursion into this seemingly incomprehensible and rather uninteresting domain by telling you a story. I had the good fortune recently of attending a seminar given by a professor of nursing. The subject matter was on doctor–nurse relationships, and we were presented with a comprehensive review of past research together with a number of suggestions for better collaboration, mutual respect and understanding. The general view was that it had been a very successful event and its subject matter became the main theme of my conversation with a medical colleague over dinner. We discussed at some length our particular notions of good doctoring and good nursing, he using his quite considerable experience of intensive care work to elaborate the key features of successful team-work, and I responding at appropriate times. From the position of believing that an effective team was primarily related to a good team leader (i.e. the doctor), we began to discuss the particular contributions of doctors and nurses in caring for patients. His observations of good nursing practices included competent technical information and the ongoing surveillance of the patient, and within this temporal commitment he noted the importance of the nurse's sensitivity to the patient's situation, their ability to interpret and understand their experiences, and their proximity to the individual's suffering and stress.

Although I could not claim that these were totally unprompted reflections on my colleague's behalf, they did illustrate that we both saw and valued similar notions of what good nursing meant. The interrogation (as he may have perceived it at first) was slowly becoming a dialogue with a much freer exchange of ideas. I heard of the stresses experienced by medical staff in such environments, their dependence on good solid nursing and their respect for the ongoing work carried out by their nursing colleagues. However, what I also heard was the still quite definitive distinction between technical and emotional care – both for doctors and nurses, and the implied need for thorough training for one and not for the other. This area, I thought to myself, could wait until the next time.

Our dinner was followed by coffee in another room, where in the rearrangement of guests I was introduced to his wife – who was also a nurse he proudly declared. Encouraged by the successful dialogue I had had with her husband I proceeded to extol the virtues of educating nurses and how important it was to the profession. She looked at me rather surprised and then announced 'Oh, I don't believe in all of that nonsense. I'm just an ordinary nurse. Anyway you don't need a lot of brains to be a good nurse. It's just basic care and common sense. I don't know why all these nurses want to go to university ... why didn't they do medicine in the first place?' I suddenly saw all my sterling efforts with this woman's husband vanish into thin air. He would never alter his basic opinion about nursing – or nurses – if his wife continued to hold and practise these sorts of ideas about her profession. I wondered how many other so-called nurses held the same view; maybe not so freely shared, but certainly with little real exploration similar views would rise to the surface. Needless to say, my new-found optimism in improved collegial relationships was short-lived. I went home cursing my own nursing colleagues.

Putting this story into the context of this paper helps to illustrate a number of important points about the way we as nurses develop an understanding of what it is we do and how we attempt to set boundaries around those meanings we have attributed to our nursing practices. The doctors wife was – on the surface – very clear about her understanding of nursing, which conformed quite rigidly to the traditional 'task duty-doctor's assistant' model that we have been struggling to get away from. Yet just because I did not happen to agree with her view of nursing – the way she chose to conceptualize it – does that necessarily mean that my view of nursing as a patient-centred ethically driven collegiate activity was any more correct, or a closer approximation to how other nurses conceptualize their work?

In trying to understand this scenario I will necessarily have to explore three areas related to the use of concepts. First, I shall explore how we use concepts in general to inform our everyday experiences. I shall then go on to look at how concepts have been formalized in nursing and caring, and thirdly I shall consider how we can use these concepts in everyday practice.

3.2 THE NATURE OF CONCEPTUALIZATION

I can remember as a student being rather disappointed by the explanation our nurse theorists used to give to the word 'concept'. It tended to go into that collection of words like variable, factor, unit, thing, or more latterly, mental image, which one had a familiarity with and was therefore able to know how to use. If a concept was a thing from which theories are built, then all things are concepts in a sense. But how do concepts differ from facts or values? When does a concept become a construct (which to the lay person seems to mean a bunch of concepts that make sense together) or indeed how do theories develop from concepts? And what about models? Could I forget all about concepts merely by saying that if we could define the meaning of words then we would not have to worry about concepts?

It was not until I had come across a little book by Wilson (1963) entitled *Thinking with Concepts* that some of these questions began to be answered. Concepts, rather than being somewhat remote esoteric notions, were at the very centre of the way we make sense of the world. They help us know what we are supposed to be doing by giving us sets of labels, which we use to create a shared or common understanding of the issue in question.

Our need for concepts in our everyday language relates to the need we have to map out the way we use, how we apply and the meaning we attach to, certain words. For example, if I asked you whether a whale, an octopus or a lobster were fishes, your judgement would be based on shared meanings of the concept 'fish'. Depending on your knowledge and past use of this concept, you would say yes or no based on reasons such as whether they lived in the sea, could swim, were cold-blooded, had scales, did not have lungs, etc. Our understanding of the concept 'fish' is limited by our current knowledge of those creatures classified within that conceptual category. If new information emerges then the concept develops to incorporate that, and so concepts help to put boundaries around words and contain the shared meanings we have of them.

Using and talking about concepts has the effect of making us self-conscious about words that we have hitherto used without thinking. We become more conscious of our actions and begin to look at them more critically, reflecting not only upon the action but also upon the significance of that action. It is altogether a different process, as we have probably come from a world of what we have called facts – e.g. that all fishes have scales and live in the sea – and where actions are performed automatically according to a routine or because of a set of values or beliefs.

Learning how to deal with concepts is more difficult than learning facts. The acquisition of facts – for example, the Latin names for the muscles in the human body – can be facilitated by understanding the order in which the muscles are identified and the sequence and use of the Latin nomenclature. However, when you try to get to grips with concepts there are no strict rules of order and discipline. Wilson has described working with concepts as being like making a map: you think you are familiar with the ground until you have to draw it. Then you begin to see where your knowledge, experience or analytical skills need to be enhanced. What is difficult for the self-conscious beginner is that questions of concept do not often have clear-cut solutions. Concepts reflect the meaning and use of words as people use them. They do not state facts, nor do they expressly uphold one particular moral view over another.

It may be useful to distinguish between these three notions of fact, value and concept. What is paramount to any explanation of concepts is the ability to spot them; for example, consider the following statements:

1.   More women are involved in caring for family members than men.
2.   Women are more caring than men.
3.   What is caring?

The first statement is one of fact: we know that more women than men look after family members in our own, and most other, societies. The second statement, in contrast, makes a claim that women are more caring than men. Although this may have some currency it is not proven, and anyone adhering to this view would be basing their argument on a set of values and beliefs. Neither of these statements should be confused with the last question, which asks 'What is caring?' This is a question of concept, in that to understand the word 'care' the individual must engage in looking critically at what care means to him, to people around him, how it is described in literature, the media, defined by scholars, and so on. A definition of caring is not what is needed, but rather a divergent exploration of how ordinary people use the word.

Being able to separate issues of fact, value and belief and concept from one another is important, as the following statement may illustrate:

'Caring is an activity that women are more naturally disposed toward and therefore women are more involved than men in caring for family members.'

We see here the combination of fact, values and concepts. In deciding whether we agree with this statement, considerations of fact and morality cannot be relevantly applied at all until one has worked out what they are supposed to apply to. Think of the doctor's wife who said that nurses did not need to be educated as nursing was just common sense. Could we begin to imagine what sort of notion she had of the concept of nursing? Was her concept of nursing consistent with what she was arguing? If you had observed her practice, would her actions also have been consistent with her conceptualization of nursing?

We are beginning to realize, rather disconcertingly, that concepts emerging from us and being formulated by us can be distorted, inaccurate, misguided, factually incorrect, value-laden, robust, comprehensive. Concepts cannot be completely fluid – like Humpty Dumpty saying that he will give his own meaning to the words – they cannot have more or less the limits one likes. Rather, the most effective use of concepts is when people pool them and all the different concepts of a thing coincide. The areas of convergence reinforce certain attributes of the conceptualization.

We may not, however, be at all inclined to engage in this sort of concept-swapping. We formulate concepts by learning to group certain features of experience together, and use certain words to describe these groupings. These broad categories are refined by the inclusion of additional features, and where possible we try to use one word to help other people get a feel of the concept. The process of forming a concept of a thing and learning the meaning of a word that describes the thing may often look the same, but in fact they are not. It is quite possible to have a concept of something but for there to exist no single word to describe it. Consider the discovery of X-rays and the new names given to describe concepts such as radiation, electricity and so on. Consider also Freud's use of words such as ego, id and superego to describe concepts related to his psychoanalytical theory.

Concept analysis is essentially an imaginative process, seen as more of an art than a science. However, the application of concepts into theoretical disciplines is the very stuff of the scientific process. Wilson uses the concept of infinity in maths to illustrate how regulated and predictable a concept can become in a discipline that is highly structured. However, in other disciplines where the social context and the attributes of the individuals using the concepts have to be taken into account, the preciseness with which concepts can be used is reduced. For example, good is a common word whose actual meaning is not governed by any complex set of formal rules; in understanding its meaning, one must be very aware of using it in particular ways and what impact it has on the individuals who use it. Concepts have both a logical and psychological dimension to them. They parallel the meaning or definition of certain words, but derive their special use from being able to map out and explain what meaning individuals attach to certain things. There is no such thing as 'the' concept of a thing – facts mop up anything that approximates a certainty in a concept. Similarly, whereas values and beliefs may influence and inform certain ways of thinking and thus identifying conceptual boundaries, we must at some stage be ready to ask ourselves why we hold a particular belief, for example, that nursing is just basic care, or that nursing is just common sense, in order to avoid becoming locked into a set of concepts that have long since passed their usefulness.

I could conclude by stating that concept formalization is much too important an activity to be given into the hands of experts. In our individual search for understanding or making sense of the world around us, we rely consciously or unconsciously on our own conceptual maps to help us. More specifically, in our understanding of our nursing practice we have built up over the years a set of ideas about nursing, caring, patients, doctors, health, suffering, illness and so on. These concepts, whether we like it or not, or whether we know it or not, influence our everyday practice in numerous subtle and quite explicit ways. They even impinge on after-dinner conversations. In order to locate some of the main thoughts and ideas within nursing that may have affected our own conceptualization of things around us, I want to trace the conceptual development as I see it within nursing and within caring. Finally I want to look at how we could use some of these ways of conceptualizing nursing and caring within our everyday practice.

3.3 HOW CONCEPTS HAVE BEEN FORMULATED IN NURSING AND CARING

How we arrive at the conceptual mix that makes up our understanding of nursing and care has been influenced by personal experience, both good and bad, our education, and a range of historical, social, political and psychological factors. The mass of knowledge available to us in books and articles acts as an intellectual trigger for our own concept formalization. However, the first point to emphasize is that each person has the task of refining and clarifying their own concepts of nursing and caring. Although we can use the conceptual frameworks and theories of people such as Henderson, Roy, Orem and Benner, it is our job to organize the information derived from these sources with what our experience tells us about the world. Of note also is the separation of the terms nursing and caring. I hope to illustrate in what follows that, while the two terms are complementary, they do not refer to the same elements. It is my argument that, in understanding how to be a good nurse, the individual must formulate a coherent and workable concept of nursing which is consistent with, and complementary to, his or her concept of caring.

A final point at this stage relates to the level of analysis. It may be slightly confusing to talk in the same breath of a concept of nursing, principles of nursing and a theory of nursing without distinguishing how we define these terms, what the relationships are and how they are used. The clarification of concepts such as nursing and caring helps the individual understand how the concepts work in practice. When workable aspects of the concepts are identified and relationships predicted, and particularly when events can be anticipated and controlled through an understanding of these relationships, then one can talk about a theory of nursing or caring. Similarly, the rules that emerge from repeated observations of the relationships between items making up the concept lead toward the formation of principles or laws. The concept of nursing therefore can and does have several theories, with their accompanying principles and rules, helping to elucidate everyday experiences for the practitioner. The fit between the theory and subsequent activity is dependent upon how consistently the implicit concept of nursing within the theory matches that of the user.

The question of whether we can survive in a pluralist nursing system with a variety of concepts and theories of nursing and caring is an interesting one, and one which I will return to later.

3.4 CONCEPT FORMALIZATION IN NURSING

In tracing the formal development of a conceptual definition of nursing it is interesting to note that the first major thrust came in the late 1940s–early 1950s in North America. Before that time, nursing was conceptualized in quite rigid ways, the Nightingale influence permeating the world to develop a system of nursing based on robust character development, the laws of hygiene and health, and strict adherence to orders passed through a female hierarchy. This particular configuration of obedience, duty, hard work and cleanliness proved to be strong in determining the way several generations of nurses chose to view themselves and their work. As Reverby (1989) notes, the strength for such an authoritarian model of nursing came from the way that it instilled idealism and pride in the skills of nursing into the majority of women. It also acted as a mechanism for virtuous women to contribute to the improvement of humanity by empowering them to care within an organizational context, rather than, as had formerly been, in the home. This movement from the home to the workplace was seen to provide women with a livelihood and independence. What is interesting is that the paternalism within the family was invariably replaced by medical paternalism.

Henderson (1964) illustrates aspects of this approach: 'My basic training was largely in a general hospital where, for the nurse, technical competence, speed of performance and a "professional" (actually an impersonal) manner were stressed. We were introduced to nursing as a series of almost unrelated procedures, beginning with making an unoccupied bed and progressing to, say, aspiration of body cavities. In this era, ability to catheterize a patient seemed to qualify a student for night duty.'

What is interesting to note from these reflections is how regimented and constrained nursing had become over the 50 years or so since it had first been formally described. Nightingale's writings belie the rigid hierarchical orientation that was to be taken, and in fact several of her own reflections on nursing are as pertinent now as they were in 1870. Reverby (1989) suggests that the stultification of nursing in these early years came about because nurses did not separate autonomy from altruism; in other words, they had unquestioningly accepted the duty to care rather than demanding the right to determine how they should satisfy that duty. Nursing had sought the linkage between autonomy and altruism, but with watered-down medical lectures as the staple diet this was rarely realized. Duty remained the basis for nursing and under these conditions nurses found it difficult to achieve the collective transition out of a woman's culture of obligation into an activist assault on the structure and beliefs oppressing them (Reverby, 1989).

The shortage of nurses after the Second World War and the developments in medical and health care technology influenced the first wave of nursing theory development in the early 1950s. The early pioneers involved in this include Henderson, Abdellah, Hall and Orem. The majority of nurse theorists between 1950 and 1980 have attempted to define the concept of nursing and operationalize it through a particular theory. A few have chosen to use the concept of caring as a way of explaining nursing, which they see as the result of caring activities (for example Leininger, Watson and Benner would tend toward this approach).

Meleis (1985) has analysed the developments in nursing theory in the period between 1950 and 1980, and has identified three main themes or schools of thought. These include needs theories, interaction theories and outcome (or holistic) theories. An analysis of developments in theories of caring (within nursing) has also been put forward here to highlight the complementary relationship between the development in nursing thought and ideas on caring. This framework has identified three main themes, comprising caring-as-duty, caring-as-therapeutic-relationships, and caring-as-an-ethical-position. Proponents of the first method include Nightingale and what can be called the 'old school'; those theorists adhering to the concept of caring-as-therapeutic-relationship include Watson, Leininger, Hall and Roach, while advocates of the final and most recent category, caring-as-ethical-position, includes notably Benner (Figures 3.1 and 3.2).

3.5 NURSING CONCEPTUALIZED AS A NEEDS-BASED THEORY

The conceptual root of the needs-based theories of Henderson, Abdellah and Orem, was Maslow's hierarchy of needs, and was influenced by Erickson's stages of development. Nursing functions were related to and determined by the needs of the patient. Physical needs were often given priority, and this tended to link the needs-based theories with the biomedical model, particularly if patient needs were related to dysfunction caused by disease or medical intervention. Although the needs-based theories did lend themselves to imaginative, independent interventions determined by nurses, the danger stalking this group of theories was the ease with which nursing interventions could be reduced to a set of actions to be performed without any wider awareness of the nurse's total role in patient care. The relative dependence of patients on the nurse to identify their needs and interpret them is also seen as a potential weakness in this set of theories.

Henderson's and Orem's theories have enjoyed widespread acceptance. Henderson's work, communicated through the ICN, has been widely adopted and adapted as manifest in Roper, Logan and Tierney's 'Activities of Daily Living Model' published in the early 1980s. Of significance to the individual nurse attempting to understand the essential elements of the needs-based concept of nursing is the amalgamation of a systematic method of analysing patient problems (the Maslow-type framework), together with a method of assessing, planning, implementing and evalu-

	Needs-based	Interactionist	Outcome (Holistic)
Major nurse theorists	Abdellah, Henderson, Orem	King, Orlando, Paterson and Zderad, Travelbee, Wiedembach	Johnson, Levine, Rogers, Roy
Paradigmatic origins	Maslow (hierarchy of needs) Erickson (dev stages) Medical model	Psychoanalytical theory Freud, Jung Psychotherapeutics Rogers: phenomenology Existentialist philosophy	General systems Social systems adaptation theory Developmental theory Symbolic interactionism
Major orientation	*Problem- focused *Focus on nurses' functions *Reductionist *Illness-based *Illness defined as deviation to be corrected	*Nursing as interpersonal process *Nurses must clarify own values *Therapeutic use of self *Humanistic not mechanistic *Illness defined as inevitable human experience from which one can grow	*Outcome of nursing care/patient expectations/goals *Interdependence of nurse/client *Client assessed within context *Focus on reestablishing harmony with environment Reestablish homoeostatic equilibrium *Illness defined as deviation in normal homoeostatic state to be corrected
Major concepts	Health, illness, needs Needs hierarchy, problems Nurse as problem-solver Nurse as decision-maker	Sensing, perceiving, validation Goal-oriented interaction Nurse as participant, partner Nurse as self-developer	Harmony with environment Stability, homoeostasis Nurse as external regulatory mechanism for clients
Deficiencies	*Clients' perception of needs not made explicit *Underdeveloped view of environment *Process of interaction not explained	*Minimum focus on biopsycho-cultural aspects of human experience *Underdeveloped view of environment	*Concepts have remained at high level of abstraction, linking utility of theories in practice *Discrete areas of nursing intervention/resp. diff to define

Figure 3.1 Conceptual framework (adapted from Meleis, 1985).

	Caring-as-duty Nightingale	Caring-as-therapeutic-relationship Leininger, Watson, Roach	Caring-as-ethical-position Benner
Major nurse theorists			
Paradigmatic origins	Judaeo–Christian theology Social mores Attitudes to women	Psychoanalysis: Freud, Jung Psychotherapy: Rogers, Mayeroff Anthropology Phenomenology: Heidegger Existentialism	Ethics: Kant, Kierkegaard Virtue ethics: MacIntyre Moral development theory: Kohlberg, Gilligan, Noddings: phenomenology - Buber
Orientation	Strict adherence to orders Concept of duty/obligation Control/subjugation of emotions Character development Accentuating professional distancing behaviours	Establish a relationship based on respect, understanding, unconditional positive regard developing skills of empathy warmth, non-judgemental attitude Viewing human experience as a phenomenological, existential spiritual experience commun-icated through caring	Contextualization of caring practices Relationship held on mutuality, trust Confidentiality, respect for persons Mutual realization empowerment
Major concepts	Devotion Dedication Unquestioning obedience Acting doing for/helping assisting Serving	Care Transpersonal care Culture Environment/health Carative factors	Support life functions/promoting health/care of body/focused attention/systematic listening/decrease sense of alienation/bear witness to human experience
Deficiencies	Denial of feelings/emotions Subjugation of self Detachment Alienation of feeling Reductionist approach	Caring still seen as technique to be mastered, a skill to be learned Well-intentioned reductionism	Difficult to attain in practice Problems of control v care and autonomy v intrusion

Figure 3.2 Conceptual framework.

ating the nursing intervention (the nursing process). Before this time, nursing activities had rarely been systematic and seldom documented in an individualized way.

3.6 THE INTERACTIONIST THEORISTS

In some sense Hildegard Peplau was seen to bridge the gap between the early needs-based theories and the interactionist theories of nursing that began to emerge in the 1960s. Peplau, a psychiatric nurse writing in 1952, based her nursing practice on a needs model but emphasized the importance of the nurse–patient relationship. The centrality of the nurse–patient relationship may have been implicit in the writings of Henderson, Abdellah and Orem, but the second wave of nurse theorists felt the need to make it central to the whole way nurses were trained to think about and carry out nursing. The focus was very much on the process of nursing: how relationships were established, how they related to the patient's wider social context, how they affected his understanding of himself and others around him, how they helped him to find a meaning for the experience of illness. Nurse theorists as diverse as King, Orlando, Travelbee and Wiedenbach can be grouped under this heading, by virtue of the fact that they were looking at the impact of the nurse on the experiences of the patient. Value clarification, understanding how to use oneself in a therapeutic way, becoming involved in patients' experiences, establishing a relationship based on trust, equality and mutual positive regard were all dimensions of nursing seen through interactionist glasses.

Nursing skills to be developed included sensitivity, perception, validation of the patient's experiences, being totally present for the other person, using intuition and subjective feelings to elucidate problems or situations that needed to be explored. Emphasis on the physical needs of patients tended to be reduced, the nurse choosing to focus first of all on the patient's experience of the situation to inform her of subsequent actions. The nursing theories within this category have been informed by such theories as Freud's and Jung's psychoanalytical theories, Roger's psychotherapeutics, and the philosophical positions of phenomenologists such as Heidegger, and existentialist philosophers, notably Teilhard de Chardin, Buber, Marcel and Nietzsche.

The development of the nursing beds at Burford Community Hospital and in Beeson Ward (Pearson 1988) could be classified as an approach to nursing drawing heavily on the interactionist framework. Current work undertaken by Ersser (1991) is attempting to uncover the therapeutic dimensions of nurse–patient interaction, and in particular focusing on the relationship existing between the specific behaviour of the nurse and patient welfare. In work so far, Ersser has identified two major factors influencing the relationship, namely, the way the nurse presents herself to the patient and how that is perceived by the patient, and secondly, the actual presence of the nurse in providing such things as contact, caring, availability, sensitivity and comfort.

A major weakness identified in this set of theories is the relative lack of attention they could be seen to devote to physical needs and the patient's need to establish positive coping behaviours to overcome the identified problem.

3.7 THE OUTCOME (HOLISTIC) THEORISTS

The relative liberation of the interactionist theories has been somewhat offset by the final wave of nursing theories to emerge in the late 1960s and early 1970s. What Meleis has called the outcome theories have emerged to provide a way of thinking about nursing which states that the goal of nursing care is to bring back some balance, stability and preservation of energy or enhancing harmony between the individual and the environment (Meleis, 1985). The best-known example of this group of theories is Roy's adaptation theory, where the nursing goal is the promotion of man's adaptation to physiological needs, self-concept, role function and interdependence. The underlying theories informing and influencing the outcome theories include general systems, adaptation and developmental theory.

The other nursing theorists include Dorothy Johnson, Martha Rogers and Myra Levine. They all see the nurse as more controlling and manipulative in determining patient outcomes, this ability being derived from the nurse's understanding of and ability to work a number of homoeostatic systems – as in Roy, using the principles of stress and adaptation to determine how to help a patient develop better coping strategies, or with Johnson's theory using the principles of behavioural systems to regulate an individual's reactions. Each theory in this category has built on the needs-based theories, and they contain within them certain subsystem aspects related to meeting physical needs. Additional elements include much more emphasis on maintaining equilibrium with the outside environment. This is seen to be achieved by the deliberate manipulation of situations, states or events in order to achieve a desired outcome.

What needs to be clarified in these theories is whether the desired outcome is arrived at jointly between the nurse and the patient, how the negotiation takes place, and what is the nature of the relationship between the nurse and the patient. The image of the nurse to emerge from these theories is one of the nurse as goal-setter, as external regulatory force to modify stimuli affecting adaptation, and as preserver of the integrity between the patient's external environment and their behaviour, perception and relations.

The outcome theories may not be seen to be a development in terms of concept formalization or clarification of roles. Indeed, as described they tend to give the impression of being mechanistic and regulated solely by the nurse. However, it may be worth pointing out that a major criticism of the theories has been their level of abstractness, making them difficult to operationalize. Thus, having the intellectual understanding of adaptation theory as it relates to self-concept is one thing, but trying to get it to work with or on a patient is something different.

It is interesting that the final wave of theories in nursing has tried to integrate man and the environment in a way that acknowledges numerous external and regulatory forces; circadian and biorhythms, energy fields and so on. It almost seems that the inward exploration enjoyed by the interactionists has moved out to legitimize the extrasensory exploration of man within his environment. Perhaps it is the combination of the inward and outward gaze that moves us on to what might be called holistic nursing theories. Certainly some of the interactionist theories, and particularly those based on existential phenomenology, e.g. Paterson and Zderad (1975) move one towards a holistic view of nursing. Similarly, an approach such as Rogers' provides a view of man that defies any attempt at crude reductionism. One could also see the sensitive and humane practitioner using Orem's theory in a manner which would recognize the open, constantly changing interaction of the individual with the internal and external environment. The question would be, which of the schools of thought would predispose toward this comprehensive view of nursing, where the emphasis would be on the need for nurses to individualize care according to the assessment of each patient.

Perhaps the issue is more about recognizing the limitations of the theory selected rather than merely going for how well it fits with one's own view of nursing. Thus in selecting and using a needs-based theory, how do I avoid making decisions for and not with patients; how do I avoid the stumbling block of laissez-faire relativism if I choose to develop an interactionist approach to nursing, and at what point does seeking to intervene in the patient's situation move from a positive intervention to one which is mechanistic, poorly conceived and potentially iatrogenic? None of these questions could ever be answered if nurses had not tried to find common meanings to the way they practised nursing. What is interesting to note is how little ideas in nursing have spread out from the first attempts of Henderson and others to describe it.

One explanation put forward here is that the relative inertia in nursing thought and concept formalization is related to the continued confusion that exists between concepts of nursing and concepts of care. What I hope to illustrate now is how the three phases of conceptualization of care as it relates to nursing help to work as a catalyst for change, and as a predictor of where nurses are in their conceptual development.

3.8 CONCEPTUAL FRAMEWORK FOR CARING

The three main phases in the development of conceptualizations in caring (as related to nursing) encompass the early image of caring-as-duty, the subsequent view of caring-as-a-therapeutic-relationship, and the most recent perspective as caring-as-ethical-position (see Figure 3.2). Ideas about caring have been intimately linked with nursing to the extent that when nursing emerged as a discrete entity at the end of the 19th century, the bedrock upon which it was based came from the strongly held views on caring, and on women's role in caring in particular.

3.8.1 Caring-as-duty

We have already mentioned Nightingale's reliance on the good character of the novice to help her become a dutiful obedient nurse. These traits were common to the 'womanly virtues' seen as intrinsically bound up with nurturing and caring. Emphasis was placed on caring as a duty, to safeguard the sick and vulnerable from unscrupulous women masquerading as nurses. The separation of the untrained, unprofessional nurses of the 19th century from the new breed of Nightingale nurses, trained, professional and obedient, reinforced the need for adherence to strong moral values.

The principles of how women should behave when caring for others have been influenced by two main forces. According to Colliere (1986) these are the caring practices that have developed in every culture, related to body practices (puberty, pregnancy, childbirth, care of newborns, care of sick, old and dying), and the effect of the Judaeo–Christian religion on the way women (in particular) care for others. What Colliere saw as a natural ecosystem of caring practices, with women developing an extensive knowledge about the body and its reactions through direct contact with the body, was slowly changed into a consecrated system where the body was seen as inherently evil and the only accepted model of care was given through religious – ergo trustworthy, devoted and obedient – women.

Colliere has described the demise of natural caring practice with its concomitant knowledge and insights, as a confiscation of women's knowledge and devaluation of women's work. This was replaced by the new religious orders of nuns, who separated off the life practices and focused on tending the sick. She goes on to claim that obedience and service were the axis of care service. Consecrated women did not have to learn to build up judgement – they had merely to learn behaviour dictated by rules.

The caring role of the woman (i.e. *nurse*) was therefore seen to have high moral or religious overtones. Anything to do with basic life events, experiences or feelings was condemned because the flesh was seen as inherently and irredeemably evil. Women's sexuality also posed a problem. Nurses were either untrustworthy, deviant and scurrilous, or they were sirens enticing young doctors away from their chosen career. How society overcame the problem of accepting women into the workforce was essentially to see them as asexual. If they were not from an actual religious order, the idea was to create a structure which promoted the same virtues. Thus devotion, dedication, vocation, obedience and submissiveness became the hallmarks of a good nurse, and also a good woman or wife.

The caring-as-duty paradigm can still be detected in some areas of nursing. Certainly the needs-based theories would have had to develop a way of altering the nurse's own perception of her caring role before she could have taken on board ideas about problem-solving, need identification and so on. This would have sounded like blasphemy to some nurses inculcated into the ways of unquestioning obedience and unthinking conformity.

3.8.2 Caring-as-therapeutic-relationship

One significant impact of the caring-as-duty paradigm was the detrimental effect it had on nurses' emotional life and self-identity. There is little record of the extent of these problems, only the effect of them in terms of high wastage rates and rapid turnover of staff. One major piece of work which brought this out in the open was Menzies' (1960) study of nurses' emotional behaviour. She found that nurses deny their feelings when dealing with patients and do not know how to resolve the subsequent emotional conflict that arises. This is turn lends to distress and disillusionment.

At the same time as Menzies' work was being discussed, a wave of development work was being done on the interactionist theories in nursing and in establishing therapeutic communities, particularly in areas of mental illness. The way caring was beginning to be described at this point was very much in psychotherapeutic terms. Rogers' (1980) seminal work on the therapeutic-use-of-self, unconditional positive regard and such techniques presupposed a more enlightened view of caring. First, caring was no longer consigned to sinners or virgins; its value was being rediscovered and was becoming a therapy that could be manipulated according to a number of humanistic principles. Mayeroff (1972), for example, identified features such as right knowledge, proper sensitivity to atmosphere and interactions, an adequate measure of patience and honesty, being able to trust the potential of others to enable them to grow, having the humility to learn from others, never giving up hope and having the courage to go on with people. The achievement of such dispositions was seen to link with self and other understanding, encouraging mutual disclosure and sharing. Suddenly, on the surface, it was acceptable to feel in nursing, it was acceptable that nurses could be seen as women and men, rather than as asexual objects.

The liberation of how nurses were to view their practices towards their patients was made explicit in a number of the interactionist theories. The implicit assumption running through these is that the nurse is able to move from what may have been an image of her caring function as determined by duty, obedience and subservience, only to be confronted with a complex set of skills to be mastered regarding empathy, sympathy, love, respect, trust and so on.

Few psychotherapeutic theories have dealt with the relationship between therapeutic relationships and physical closeness – one of the few combinations that distinguish nursing therapeutic relationships from other types. Again, the idea that caring is based on the mutual understanding and acceptance of two people is tolerable when timetables limit the contact period, or when clothes and covers separate the talk from the body, but in situations where intimate procedures are performed by a carer (nurse or other) the meaning of therapeutic must be more than a gesture.

Leininger and Watson are among a few nurse theorists to develop a theory of nursing from a standpoint of describing caring practices. Leininger (1978) holds that nursing is a learned humanistic art and science that focuses upon personal caring behaviours, functions and processes, directed toward promoting and maintaining health behaviours or recovery from illness. She sees care as essential for the development, health maintenance and survival of humans, the behaviours, expression and pattern of which serve society to prevent human misery and alleviate stress and socially disruptive conditions. Her view that caring is culturally determined, with a number of universal and specific caring practices emerging from different societies, is reminiscent of Colliere's explanation of the origins of caring practices. Leininger, however, does not identify duty as the motivating factor in ensuring that caring takes place; rather, she sees caring as a integral part of cultural life which people learn how to do. She does not particularly stress the therapeutic nature of caring, giving it a more universal role. However, the list of personal attributes she has identified as necessary for caring do link her work with psychotherapeutic literature. Personal attributes of the carer include compassion, empathy, helping and coping behaviours, stress-alleviating measures, touching, (hand/body contact) nurturance, succouring, surveillance, protective, restorative and stimulating behaviours, health maintenance, instruction and consultation.

Watson's (1985) work begins to move from a caring-as-therapeutic-relationship paradigm to a caring-as-ethical position. She describes it as phenomenological, existentialist and spiritual in nature, the goal of which is to assist the person being cared for to attain a higher level of harmony in mind, body and soul. This is achieved through caring which requires knowledge, a moral commitment to human values and the ability to use what Watson calls carative factors. These range from forming a therapeutic relationship, helping the individual get a meaning from the situation, promoting feelings such as security, hope, and courage, to meeting basic needs and teaching the patient. In some ways it is difficult to see how Watson's interpretation differs from the humanistic nursing theory of Paterson and Zderad. She seems to be using the concept of care as a medium for explaining how the nurse should behave, i.e. acting as a moral agent, and what she should do, i.e. engaging in caring transactions. This, however, is never explicitly stated. Certainly, descriptions of the 10 carative factors and how the nurse uses them puts the work into the caring-as-therapuetic-relationship category.

3.8.3 Caring-as-ethical position

The final category highlights particularly the work of Benner. Within her discussion of developing expert practitioners, Benner outlines a notion of caring which has its roots in ethical theories and phenomenological theories of moral development. Benner's work reflects a growing interest in value clarification and virtue ethics in general (MacIntyre, Foot), as well as discussions relating to ethical development (notably Kohlberg, Perry and Gilligan). Benner argues for the contextualization of caring practices with the focus being on health promotion rather than illness, the empowering of nurses to care for patients as they see appropriate; being able to do this in an environment that protects and values caring practices; understanding the balance between autonomy and altruism; and finally, being able to demonstrate the benefits this sort of care has for patients.

The sort of ethical stance taken to achieve this is not bounded by rules or codes of conduct. A much more stringent test is required – that of the individual practitioner having to make independent judgements on each case within the context of where the care is carried out. This level of ethical decision-making is seen as the most advanced and requires experience and the ability to learn from that experience.

Caring practices are seen as grounded in the shared experiences of the nurse and the patient. The nurse is equipped to make good decisions and correct judgements because of her ethical stance; she is also equipped to perform a number of caring activities with the patient – supporting life functions, promoting health, care of the body, being able to give focused attention, listen systematically, coach her patient, foster a healing relationship, decrease the patient's sense of alienation and being present or being a witness to their human experiences.

Some of these skills are similar to therapeutic skills; the perceived difference, however, lies in the way the nurse chooses to use them; in the therapeutic paradigm a number of rules and principles would come into play, while in the ethical paradigm the nurse responds to the patient as a person and establishes a caring relationship based on mutual realization. The central tenet of this relationship is the engagement of the two people. While the therapeutic caring relationship may claim the same features, again the distinction is in relation to how the nurse decides what to do, how engaged she becomes and how authentic her communication is with the other person.

The ethical position for caring relationships has also been explored by Noddings (1984). She views caring as a universal attribute which is influenced by each person's memory of caring and being cared for. Our search for caring arises out of our ideal notion of what caring should be like, and we strive to perfect our relationships through understanding how to move from self-centredness to other-centredness. Caring, according to Noddings, requires emotional displacement and engrossment, tuning in to the same wavelength as the other person and wanting to get involved with them. Elsewhere (Kitson, 1987) I have identified three key aspects of the nurse's caring function. They include having the appropriate skills and knowledge, having a commitment to care for the other person and respecting the other person's wishes, desires and rights. These features reflect both Benner's and Noddings' notions of mutual realization, motivational displacement and engrossment.

Certainly the caring-as-ethical position demands a comprehensive view of the patient and an autonomy for nursing decision-making and action rarely found. It may be that the caring-as-ethical position could transform any of the nursing theories previously described into holistic models of nursing care. What I now want to explore is what happens when you link the two models together.

3.9 USING CONCEPTS OF NURSING AND CARING

The question now arising is whether certain nursing theories are more naturally linked with ways of viewing caring than are others. Figure 3.3 summarizes how the two ideas might be linked. Here we see a matrix where caring-as-duty naturally occurs with the needs-based nursing models; caring-as-therapeutic intervention would tend to connect with interactionist models, and the caring-as-ethical position would relate to the outcome model as defined in its broadest, holistic terms. However, it may also be appropriate to argue that there is no intellectual refinement or development from needs-based to holistic nursing theories; they each have merit and are all still appropriate. In this case, the caring paradigms would determine the internal consistency or appropriateness of each theory. For example, it would be in everyone's best interests to move nurses' views of caring from duty-based to the therapeutic or the ethical position. Each of the theories would be able to identify what caring would be like conceptualized as duty, therapy or ethical stance. It is important for the practitioner to know how to move from one way of thinking to the other.

If we think that intellectual and ethical development in nursing and caring not only moves from duty to ethics but from needs to holistic nursing then we have a more interesting journey to plot in terms of concept formalization and the sharing and interpretation of those concepts. For example, I could argue that my doctor's wife was still operating on the needs-based, caring-as-duty notion of nursing. In the 20 years or so of her nursing career she had never discarded the traditional values. The issue then would be to try to move her down through the caring dimensions of the model or across the nursing theories. I could, of course, go

Caring	Needs-based nursing theory	Interactionist (holistic)	Outcome (holistic)
Duty	*Task-orientated *Subservient	*Nurse not authentically engaged *One-way communication *'Phoney' relationship	*Rule-based *Inauthentic *Mechanistic care
Therapeutic relationships	*Care more individualized *Nurse more involved in establishing patient's view of situation *May tend towards routine interactions	*Nurse authentically engaged *Consistency between theory and mode of behaviour	*Using range of therapeutic skills to achieve desired outcomes *Patient actively involved in decision-making *Tending to follow prescribed patterns of therapeutics
Ethical position	*Problem-solving, patient-centred approach *Nurse actively involving patient in decisions *Possibly lacking therapeutic skills to deal with extreme emotional situations e.g. feelings of anger, guilt	*Nurse authentically engaged *Using context to make decisions in addition to therapeutic skills *May lack understanding of wider contextual issues	*Seeing person in context *Relationship built on mutuality, equity, trust *Nurse making independent autonomous decisions about care

Figure 3.3 Nursing and caring conceptual framework.

diagonally and end up (where the professor of nursing would claim to be) in the caring-as-ethical position, holistic nursing box. Here we would expect to find what Benner would call expert, or advanced, practitioners.

An important addition in this proposed conceptual framework would be to attempt to offer case studies of nursing interventions reflecting elements of the proposed combinations. By doing this we may find that our notions of caring and nursing, separate and together, influence the way we interact with our patients. No matter what happens, though, I think we would all agree that a stark needs-based model of nursing based on caring-as-duty is definitely passé. That paradigm has certainly shifted ... or has it really?

POINTS FOR DISCUSSION

Kitson's paper traced how concepts such as caring and nursing have been influenced by a number of nurse theorists who, by selecting combinations of more general theories from disciplines such as philosophy, physiology, general systems theory and psychotherapeutics, have constructed ways of explaining what nurses do. The main trends in the conceptual development of nursing and caring were divided into three main phases, reflecting the major orientation of the ideas bounding the particular view of nursing and caring.

The main point of the paper was to map out some sort of relationship between the thinking on nursing and on caring, and to argue that practitioners must become aware of their own conceptual position in order to provide a service that shows consistency between how they think about what they do and what they actually do. The paper provoked a lot of discussion, particularly in relation to the robustness of the caring–nursing framework as outlined in Figure 3.3. There was a general dislike of the notion that individuals could be located on a 3 × 3 matrix where their view of nursing and caring could be explained. This unease with the deductive approach to explaining nursing realities was commented on by one participant, who said that a lot of confusion already existing in nursing regarding theories and models was exactly because academic theorists chose to analyse nursing without taking sufficient time to generate knowledge inductively, or by detailed observation of everyday events.

Questions surrounding the reliability and validity of the proposed framework accounted for a lot of the debate: for example, how do we know that moving from a needs-based, caring-as-duty approach (the top left hand corner of Figure 3.3) to a holistic, caring-as-ethical position approach (the bottom right-hand corner of Figure 3.3) is any better for the patient? Kitson defended the model by saying that it was an attempt to organize and sort a range of concepts about nursing and caring which hitherto had not been analysed. The model was being offered for practitioners to decide whether it had any merit or not. It was a mechanism for helping nurses think about how and what they thought about nursing and what their understanding of caring was.

Another problem identified was that, for the most part, nurses do not find any of the nursing theories or models useful in their everyday practice, and therefore any way of trying to explain their conceptual development in nursing by using such theories is in itself redundant. The response of this was, why then teach such models if they are useless – and more importantly, what are the basic concepts that the majority of nurses use to inform them about their everyday practice? There was widespread agreement from the group that nursing thought in general was quite incomprehensible to other professionals. The reason for this was not clear, but it was agreed that more practical steps should be taken to begin to clearly explain the shared meanings that nurses hold about the way they practise.

A number of sociopolitical issues affecting the conceptualization of nursing and caring were also touched on in the discussion. Notably this included race and gender issues, particularly with reference to the power that such groups held within health care organizations to influence the way that people thought about and practised their work. Was there any point in trying to move nursing towards an independent autonomous profession by giving practitioners the conceptual framework to help them nurse their patients in a way that was not solely dictated by medical orders or a sense of duty? Would the patient be any better off? The reality still seems to be that for the most part nursing is carried out in this way, so are the overriding concepts determining nursing thinking more accurately characterized by the doctor's wife who said it was really just common sense?

The discussion finished off by reflecting on this point and saying that until we understood what common sense consisted of, we could not say whether we would want to support this notion or not. Certainly, the intellectualization of nursing for its own sake was totally rejected as this was seen (and people had provided the experience of it) as being highly divisive and destructive to helping nurses provide better care.

REFERENCES

Abdellah, F. G., Beland, I. L., Martin, A., Matheney, R. V. (1973) *New Directions in Patient-Centred Nursing: Guidelines for Systems of Service, Education and Research*, Macmillan, New York.

Benner, P. (1984) *From Novice to Expert*, Addison-Wesley, Reading, Mass.

Brooks, J. A. (1983) Evolution of a definition of nursing. *Advances in Nursing Science*, July 51–85.

Buber, M. (1958) *I and Thou*, 2nd edn, Charles Schribner and Sons, New York.

Colliere, M. F. (1986) Invisible care and invisible woman as health-care providers. *International Journal of Nursing Studies*, **23** (2), 95–112.

Erickson, E. H. (1953) Growth and crises of the health personality, in *Personality in Nature, Society and Culture*, (eds Lluckhohn and Murray) Alfore Knopf, New York.

Ersser, S. (1991) A search for the therapeutic dimensions of nurse–patient interaction, in *Nursing as Therapy*, eds A. Pearson, R. McMahon, Chapman and Hall, London.

Foot, P. (1978) *Virtues and Vices*, Blackwell, Oxford.

Freud, S. (1969) *An Outline of Psychoanalysis*, W W Norton, New York.

Gilligan, C. (1982) *In a Different Voice: Psychological Theory and Women's Development*, Harvard University Press, Harvard.

Hall, B. A. (1977) The effect of interpersonal attraction on the therapeutic relationship: a review and suggestion for further study. *Journal of Psychiatric Nursing*, **15** (9), 18–23.

Heidegger, M. (1962) *Being and Time*, Harper and Row, London.

Henderson, V. (1966) *The Nature of Nursing*, Macmillan, New York.

Johnson, D. E. (1980) The behavioural system model for nursing, in *Conceptual Models for Nursing Practice*, (eds J. P. Riehl and C. Roy) Appleton-Century-Crofts, New York.

King, I. M. (1981) *A Theory for Nursing: Systems, Concepts, Process*, John Wiley and Sons, New York.

Kohlberg, L. (1969) State and sequence: the cognitive–developmental approach to socialisation, in *Handbook of Socialisation Theory and Research* (ed. D. Goshin) Rand McNally, Chicago.

Kitson, A. L. (1987) A comparative analysis of lay caring and professional (nursing) caring relationships. *International Journal of Nursing Studies*, **24** (2), 155–165.

Leininger, M. (1978) *Transcultural Nursing: Concepts, Theories and Practices* Wiley, New York.

Levine, M. E. (1973) *Introduction to Clinical Nursing*, 2nd edn, F. A. Davis, Philadelphia.

MacIntyre, A. (1981) *After Virtue*, Notre Dame, University of Notre Dame Press.

Marcel, G. (1965) *Being and Having: an Existentialist Diary*, Harper Torchbooks, Harper and Row, New York.

Maslow, A. H. (1954) *Motivation and Personality*, Harper and Row, New York.

Mayeroff, M. (1972) *On Caring*, Harper and Row, New York.

Meleis, A. (1985) *Theoretical Nursing: Development and Progress*, J B Lippincott and Co, Philadelphia.

Menzies, I. (1960) *A Case Study in the Functioning of Social Systems as a Defence Against Anxiety*, Tavistock, London.

Nietzsche, F. (1954) *The Portable Nietzsche* (ed W. Kaufman), Viking Press Inc, New York.

Nightingale, F. (1989) *Notes on Nursing, What it is and What it is Not*, Harrison, London.

Noddings, N. (1984) *Caring: a Feminine Approach to Ethics and Moral Education.* University of California Press, Berkeley California.

Orem, D. E. (1980) *Nursing: Concepts of Practice*, 2nd edn, McGraw-Hill, New York.

Orlando, I. (1961) *The Dynamic Nurse–Patient Relationship*, G P Putnam's Sons, New York.

Paterson, J. G., Zderad, L. T. (1976) *Humanistic Nursing*, Wiley, New York.

Pearson, A. (1988) *Primary Nursing: Nursing in the Burford and Oxford Nursing Development Units*, Croom Helm, London.

Perry, W. B. (1968) *Forms of Intellectual and Ethical Development in the College Years: a Scheme*, Holt Reinhart and Winston.

Peplau, H. (1952) *Interpersonal Relations in Nursing*, G P Putnam's Sons, New York.

Reverby, S. (1989) A caring dilemma: womanhood and nursing in historical perspective, in *Contemporary Leadership Behaviour* 3rd ed. (eds E. C. Hein and M. J. Nicholson) Scott, Foresman/Little Brown Higher Ed, Illinois.

Roach, M. S. (1984) *Caring: The Human Mode of Being Implications for Nursing.* Perspectives in Caring, Monograph 1, University of Toronto, Toronto.

Rogers, M. (1980) Nursing: a science of unitary man, in *Conceptual Models for Nursing Practice*, (eds J. P. Rheil and C. Roy) Appleton-Century-Crofts, New York.

Roper, N., Logan, W. Tierney, A. (1980) *The Elements of Nursing*, Churchill Livingston, Edinburgh.

Roy, C. (1976) *Introduction to Nursing. An adaptation model*. Prentice-Hall, Eaglewood Cliffs.

Teilhard de Chardin, P. (1967) *On Love*, Harper and Row, New York.

Travelbee, J. (1971) *Interpersonal Aspects of Nursing*, 2nd edn, F A Davis, Philadelphia.

Watson, J. (1985) *Nursing: Human Science and Human Care*, Appleton-Century-Crofts, Norwalk.

Wiedenbach, E. (1964) *Clinical Nursing: A Helping Art*, Springer-Verlag, New York.

Wilson, J. (1963) *Thinking with Concepts*, Cambridge University Press, Cambridge.

4

Decorous didactics: early explorations in the art and science of caring, circa 1860–90

Anne-Marie Rafferty

4.1 INTRODUCTION

Nursing reform in 19th-century civilian hospitals was the product of a complex set of pressures in which doctors, administrators and nurses perceived the benefits of reform in different ways. In this chapter it is argued that the hospital can be considered a microcosm of society, and that the content and conduct of programmes in nurse training reflected contemporary ambivalence towards expanding educational opportunities for women. The question of whether nursing was an art or a science lay at the heart of a wider debate on the occupational status and qualifications for nursing during the latter part of the 19th century. The view that nursing was essentially an art and a 'calling', was championed by Nightingale. Mrs Bedford Fenwick and her allies insisted that nursing, like other professions, was a 'scientific' and technical enterprise. The conflict between these two opposing positions was most dramatically displayed during the nurses' registration debate. This chapter considers the arguments of the key actors in the discourse.

4.2 CLINICAL CAREERISM

The reform of nursing from the mid-19th century was more an attempt to gradually improve the calibre of recruits rather than to radically reconstruct the health care division of labour. As a 'museum' of clinical material, the hospital came to occupy a central position in the reform of medicine and nursing. The increasing sophistication of scientific knowledge has been invoked as the source for generating the demand for a competent observer to supervise and observe patients in the doctor's absence (Abel-Smith, 1964; Petersen, 1978). Doctors, however, were only ever intermittently present in hospital wards since they undertook private work to compensate for honorary appointments with voluntary hospitals. To the extent that nursing work was perceived as providing continuous patient supervision, the development of training can be considered as driven more by economic than epistemological concerns.

The hospital was not only a catalyst for medical careers but a stage upon which new social roles were explored and negotiated (Rosenberg, 1987; Reverby, 1987; Gamarnikov, 1985; Holden and Littlewood, 1991). As a microcosm of society, however, the hospital was constrained in the range and repertoire of relationships it could import and export. Elaborating existing social arrangements therefore created minimal disruption to established labour relations. Nursing work was acceptable as a form of employment since it merely extended women's domestic role into the public domain. Summers (1988) argues that it was women's relations with their servants which provided the basis for transferring middle-class authority relations and influence to society at large. 'Ladies' were supposed to exercise moral supervision over female members of the lower classes, teaching them cleanliness, discipline and respect for their employers' way of life. From a managerial point of view, women were perceived as less assertive, more biddable and more compliant than men; hence translocating the domestic hierarchy constituted not only managerial but economic sense (Hogg, 1967).

Reforming nursing had other advantages. Hospitals were considered as places to be feared rather than revered. Indeed, the hospital was so closely associated with infection that the term 'hospitalism' was used to denote morbidity and mortality associated with erysipelas and other hospital-borne fever (Rosenberg, 1987). The stigma attached to workhouse infirmaries was the extreme form of opprobrium attached to all institutions (Pinchbeck, 1985). Administrators perceived nurses as allies in reconstructing the reputations and economic viability of the institutions in which they served and managed (Maggs, 1987). Reformed nurses could therefore be converted into the marketing material for the new institutional image-builders to mould.

4.3 TRAINING TRANSITIONS

The new occupational roles which were emerging in the new hospital division of labour required definition. Training provided one means of institutionalizing a stable and hierarchically arranged division of labour. The reform of nursing hinged upon adapting the character and attitudes of the 'new' nurses to the routine and disciplined order of the hospital. The reformed nurse had to absorb a new culture, a new set of norms and regulations; the old culture of casual and supernumerary work was to be replaced with regularity and routine (Baly, 1986). Fixed hours of work partly dictated the characteristics of the labour force required for recruitment. The new generation of labour was one which could commit itself to the new culture of the hospital and continuity of care. This automatically excluded women with family responsibilities, and implied the recruiting of younger, more pliable nurses (Reverby, 1987; Robinson and Rafferty, 1988).

4.4 MORAL MATTERS

Although Nightingale was by no means the earliest exponent and author on training for nurses, she is indubitably its most famous (Williams, 1980). Baly argues that Miss Nightingale regarded nurse training not as an 'educational' but as a 'moral' process, involving the development of character and self-control rather than academic training (Baly, 1986). Nightingale's 'moral' theory was consistent with contemporary educational theory, which emphasized the development of 'character' as well as habits of thought.

Nightingale's view of nurse training as a moral process can be further explained by her 'organismic' view of hospital structure and function. Rosenberg argues that Nightingale perceived the hospital as a 'moral' universe in which the microcosmic body interacted dynamically with the macrocosmic environment (Rosenberg, 1979). This 'holistic' approach to disease aetiology and pathology broke down distinctions between the physical and the moral, the mind and the body: all were subsumed within the 'moral'. Control of disease implied control of the 'environment', and this was interpreted broadly to include the physical and spiritual, human, hospital and external environments. Nursing was concerned with regulating those environments and placing the body in the best circumstances for nature to act upon it. The correlation between the moral order of the hospital and society was axiomatic to Nightingale. Filth and contamination represented states of moral distance from God which required intervention: cleanliness was literally next to Godliness. The laws of God were revealed in nature as the laws governing health and disease, and it was one's Christian duty to observe and respond to such laws.

Nightingale was sensitive to the correlation between poverty and disease, but her solutions were individualistic and fatalistic rather than politically radical. If people failed to obey the dictates of God inherent within the organization of their bodies, they could only expect disease. If a hospital were contaminated by filth, administrative irresponsibility and immorality, fevers and infections were inevitable (Rosenberg, 1979). Rosenberg attributes Nightingale's denial of the specific nature of disease and her commitment to the 'zymotic' theory of disease aetiology and transmission to the influence of William Farr. Farr was a medical statistician and the Compiler of Abstracts in the Registrar-General's office. He was a close acquaintance of Miss Nightingale. Farr believed that 'zymosis' produced disease in a manner similar to fermentation, hence small quantities of 'poison' could produce widespread atmospheric contamination

(Guler, 1979). Nightingale's reference to the nursing care of patients is usually made in the context of her views on contagion.

4.5 PEDAGOGY AND PROPRIETY

Nightingale's views on training were shaped not only by her ideas on disease aetiology but by her perceptions of the role and status of women within the hospital social hierarchy (Showalter, 1981). The importance she attached to self-control and discipline in training can be understood as an attempt to ensure decorous conduct between men and women of different social classes in an evolving social environment. Moral purity was a primary prerequisite of nursing. A nurse should first and foremost, however, be a 'good woman', she must be…'Chaste, in the sense of the Sermon on the Mount; a good nurse should be the "Sermon on the Mount" in herself' (Quain, 1982). 'Immodest carelessness' was the main impediment to the performance of the proper duties of the nurse. Men were portrayed as moral sensors and censors of women's conduct, tuned to the merest hint of moral laxity in women. Attitudes such as these were used to legitimize men's right to supervise and superintend the behaviour of women. Nurses were judged according to the same double standard of Victorian morality which applied to all women: they were considered the morally vulnerable yet culpable partner in the hospitalized coupling of science and sensitivity (Trudgill, 1976).

4.6 DATA OF DISTINCTION

The emphasis on self-control in nurse training can be traced directly to contemporary constructions of gender. Discussion concerning the differences between the intellectual characteristics of men and women had been conducted at the level of moral prescription, with only limited appeal to empirical evidence. The application of concepts derived from Darwinian evolutionary biology to the question of gender differences located the debate in a morally resonant and scientifically constructed discourse. The debate on gender was a response to challenges made to contemporary social prescriptions that defined women in terms of their biological functions. This deterministic mode of thinking applied to both men and women, but with different effects: like society, nature was also hierarchically ordered. Women's physiological fluctuations and frailty were evidence of their emotional, psychological and political instability. Representations of women as labile, unpredictable and unstable beings justified their exclusion from emotionally, politically and intellectually demanding activities. The physiological flux of menstruation, the delicacy of the 'weaker' sex and her reproductive functions, justified her exclusion from the public world of work, and dictated that she confine her ambitions to the domestic sphere. Men, by contrast, being physically stronger, were considered fitter in all respects, hence their right to participate in all spheres closed to women.

It was those functions that derived immediately and directly from women's reproductive and domestic 'missions' that defined her supremacy. Yet as the antithesis of the workplace and as an area which consumed rather than produced resources, the status of the home was low in comparison to the material world of work. Women's reproductive and physiological frailty was taken as proof of their incapacity to operate in a consistent and stable manner in the public sphere. Women's superior moral status, however, was not universally given but a product of superior social status. Those less fortunate and socially advantaged could acquire a sense of cultivation through the exercise of discipline and self-control.

The proximity of nurses to patients meant that they were ideally placed to influence the moral welfare of those in their care; control of self implied the capacity to exercise control over others. The recruitment of 'ladies' to nursing was not perceived by Nightingale as the sole solution to strengthening the moral 'fibre' of patients: she was adamant that women accustomed to hard work should constitute the basis of the workforce. The demand for ladies to occupy positions of superintendence was also considered great, but the prime qualification for this office was a practical acquaintance with every detail of a nurse's work and personal knowledge of every branch of it. To this end there was little more likely to bring discredit upon ladies nursing than superficial knowledge; a full and thorough experience was what was required for superintendence.

4.7 SCHOOLING IN HEALTH

Nightingale conceived of nurse training schools as 'normal' schools and wrote of a tripartite structure in the staffing of the training school. The trained 'home-sister', or class mistress, would teach and drill the probationers in the medical instructor's lectures. She would also give singing and Bible classes and liaise with ward sisters on probationers' progress. Ward sisters would be responsible for the ward instruction of the nurses, and medical instructors for lecturing on the nursing aspects of medicine and surgery, of prescribing reading and examining the work of probationers. Baly has referred to this as the 'tripod' of nurse training, backed up by the probationers taking case notes and keeping diaries (Baly, 1984).

Moral supervision and the moral welfare of probationers was crucial, and Nightingale suggested that hospitals be built with such matters in mind. She recommended that nurses should be assigned to self-contained wards to discourage gossiping and consorting with medical students, and to prevent mischief-making between wards. The whole establishment was to be constructed so that the probationers' dining rooms, day rooms and dormitories and the matron's residence and office were together, and '... the probationers under the matron's immediate hourly inspection and control ...' (Nightingale, 1883) The Home Sister's watchful eye ensured that pastoral duties were combined with tutorials. The provision of supervision from a single vantage point was the key constituent of Nightingale's organizational aesthetic.

4.8 KNOWING 'BY HEART'

The roots of education as character training can also be located in wider perceptions of women as repositories of virtue and guardians of morality in the home and family. The cult of domesticity celebrated by the Victorians transformed the home into a sanctuary sealed off from the sullying sins of the secular world. In a world of squalor and congestion, the home provided a refuge from the moral maladies of society. Women as moral supremacists were idealized in the medical and Romantic literature of the period as the saviours of a society threatened with immorality, materialism and irreligion. Education provided the means of inculcating women with the values of wifely and maternal duties, and a vehicle for combating the moral decadence of working class behaviour generally. Inasmuch as women were praised for their management of the moral condition of society, they were also condemned for its failure.

The domestic ideology derived from the 'separate spheres' theory of a gendered division of labour in which mens' and women's roles were separate but complementary (Hall, 1979). Separation of the two spheres was considered crucial to social 'progress' and stability. Separate spheres for the sexes was justified as a 'natural' division of labour based on biological characteristics and capabilities. In the case of women, their social functions were defined by their reproductive capabilities, which justified their confinement to wifely and child-rearing duties. Women were held responsible for the moral and physical welfare of children, the family, and ultimately the nation, but lacked the authority to determine the conditions under which their duties might be properly discharged (Darin, 1978; Lewis, 1980). Men as physically and constitutionally stronger were duty-bound to protect the 'weaker sex', legally and politically. If women benefited from their role as the physical and moral regenerators of society, they were also burdened with the responsibilities attached to that role.

The contradictions inherent within the domestic ideology nevertheless did little to undermine the power of the ideology. From the middle to the end of the 19th century there was considerable opposition to improving the intellectual content of educational provision for working and middle class women (Digby, 1978). The employment pattern for many working women demanded domestic rather than literacy skills for successful performance (Burstyn, 1983; Purvis, 1981). The design and determination of curricula was consistently dominated by the desire to prepare girls for their role as wives and mothers, rather than for independent careers.

4.9 QUALIFYING CHARACTER

The qualifications of a nurse therefore were defined in terms of character, not intellect. A good nurse could not be produced from bad material asserted one contemporary: as well as being sober, truthful and upright, with a fair amount of education and plenty of sound common sense, a nurse was expected to be a good disciplinarian, firm yet gentle in her manner, willing to be taught, and devoted to her work (Benton, 1877). The slightest 'stain' on her character should exclude a woman from being raised to the high office of the nurse. Her manner should convey the impression that it is in the sickroom where she finds her appointed field of sacrifice and sacred duty (Barwell, 1857). The nurse was portrayed by reformers as an agent of the socialization and 'civilization' of patients. To this end, training schools attempted to 'elevate' their incumbents in the hope that this 'superior' social influence could be passed on to patients. It was important that nurses, and especially those originating from the same class as their charges, should no longer identify with a working-class culture, widely disparaged and despised in the polemics of pedagogy. The ward became a focus for new forms of moral and spiritual stewardship, in which nurses acted as 'missioners' of physical and moral health.

4.10 EMPIRICAL EXAMINATION

'Character' rather than theory or intellectual talents became the touch-stone of nursing skill and qualifications. Nurse training as 'character' training legitimized rather than challenged established authority relations in hospitals. Nightingale insisted that nursing was an art and a calling, practised by women under scientific heads, i.e. physicians and surgeons (Nightingale, 1894). As an art, Nightingale felt that nursing proper could only be taught at the bedside and in the sickroom or ward. Lectures and books were valuable accessories, but these had to be supplemented by an apprenticeship. The danger of the contemporary faith in 'literary educa-tion and colleges for women', according to Nightingale, was the fallacy that everything could be taught by books and lectures and that memory provided the 'great step to excellence'. 'Character' and practical ability were the foremost tests of nursing. Nursing was an art, but one requiring practical and scientific training. As an art, it could only be tested by its results, by the work done and concurrent supervision (Nightingale, 1894).

The emphasis on training objectives shifted in the last 40 years of the 19th century from an essentialist view of moral and character training to a professional one. The new nursing elite that emerged from the first wave of nursing reform looked to medicine for inspiration in developing a model of professional organization for nurses. Attempts to realize their aspirations generated tensions between the new nurses and the stakehold-ers of health care. Not all agreed with the role prescribed by Nightingale.

Imbued with the spirit of suffragism and the desire to carve out independent careers for educated women, the 'new' nurses strove for freedom and
mobility in the health care market. They were not satisfied with the place
allotted to them by the stakeholders and statesmen of health care, and
strove to define their own occupational territory. Expanding employment
opportunities for women provided an entrée into the public arena from
which they had hitherto been excluded. In their bid for professional status,
the 'new' nurses looked towards medicine for a model to emulate. Assuming the mantle of medicine meant, however, identifying closer with medical interests, values and practices.

4.11 REGISTERING DIFFERENCES

It was the representation of nursing as a profession analogous to medicine
that divided Fenwick and her allies from Nightingale and her supporters.
Nightingale did not participate publicly in what became the nurses' registration debate, but her clandestine contribution is nevertheless evident
from the arguments used by her supporters. The debate on registration
revolved around those who wished to reconstruct nursing as a free profession, controlling its own fees and conditions of service, and those who
wished to maintain the dominance of hospital management interests in
determining the conditions of service. Fenwick argued for the emancipa-
tion of nurses and nurse training from the control of the hospitals. This
was necessary to protect the public and 'thoroughly' trained nurses from
incompetent nurses. The public had no protection against the nurse who
had acquired a hospital certificate and subsequently proved to be incompetent. No hospital, it was argued, was responsible for a nurse once she
had left its service. Initially, Fenwick proposed that the organization she
had helped to establish, the British Nurses' Association, should 'register'
nurses. Later, proposals for a state-backed system of credentials with a
general nursing council were adopted as the official policy of the Association
(Abel-Smith, 1960; Dingwall *et al.*, 1988). The council would be responsible
to the general body of nurses and the public for preventing from working
any woman who proved herself unworthy of trust (Fenwick, 1890).

The implication of state involvement in training matters was perceived
as a threat to the economic interests of the prestigious voluntary hospitals,
which relied upon their antique reputations and venerable status to attract
funds and recruits. State registration implied a depreciation of hospital
training and the value of hospital certificates and testimonials to the
careers of recruits. Fenwick and her allies were anxious to break the
particularistic power of the hospital, and argued that nursing should be
constituted and legally recognized as a distinct profession, with a central
controlling body of its own along the same lines as the medical profession
(Fenwick, 1892). Any proposal that nurses might be registered by a 'foreign body' outside the hospital was, however, rejected by Nightingale, as

such an intervention was likely to interfere with the conventual discipline and esprit de corps so essential to maintaining the high ideals of nursing as a calling.

4.12 TECHNICAL DISAGREEMENTS

Fenwick rejected the exclusive emphasis on the personal qualities of the nurse as the key to qualification. In arguing for technical competence, she was not denigrating those qualities but argued that the accomplished nurse should ideally combine the strengths of the female medical student and the ministering angel. No attempt was made to register the qualities required to make a perfect nurse (Fenwick, 1892).

Opponents of registration for nurses rejected any claim for analogy and by implication, intellectual and social parity, with medicine. The value of a medical man lay primarily in his 'scientific' skill and knowledge and ability. That he should also be a man of high character and good manners was desirable, but a man defective in those particulars might still make an excellent physician or surgeon. The doctor's function was primarily scientific and his qualifications intellectual. These could be measured with intellectual tests and the result recorded on the professional register (Bonham-Carter, 1892). By contrast, nursing was qualitatively different and 'good' nursing could not be tested by examination (Rathbone, 1892).

The question of the relative weight that should be attached to technical and moral qualifications provided the fulcrum for the registration debate. Technical knowledge for nurses was considered subordinate to personal character by antiregistrationists (Burdett Papers, 1909). Lavinia Dock, a close associate of Fenwick and a leader of American nursing, railed against the resistance to considering nurse training as a form of 'technical' training (Nutting and Dock, 1907; Breay and Fenwick, 1928; Rafferty, 1989). Dock defined technical training as the 'training of hand and brain in harmonious duet', and was highly critical of the aversion to technical or manual training in nursing (Dock, 1905). Not only did she argue that such thinking was out of step with modern educational thinking, but far from being antagonistic to character training, technical education was of supreme value in character forming. Indeed, technical education could even be conceived of as a corrective to such modern 'defects' of character as idleness, indefinite purpose, aimlessness and useless occupation. Far from perceiving 'character' and 'technical' training as dichotomous, Dock warned against any artificial separation of the two (Dock, 1905).

4.13 CONCLUSION

Victorian Britain has been characterized as a period of moral crisis in which women were expected to perform as the barometers and bearers of moral standards. Anti-intellectualism and the 'separate spheres' ideology reinforced fears that nurses were developing ideas above their station (Holland, 1904). The pro-registrationist challenge was perceived as a threat, not simply to social relations between doctors and nurses, but to the gender order of health care generally. The emphasis on 'character' training in nursing reinforced the anti-intellectualism which justified the exclusion of women from professional work. Nurse reformers, committed to a professional model for nursing, distanced themselves from character training by adopting a strategy based on a technical and scientific approach derived from medicine. The implications of applying a medical model of organization to further the autonomy of nurses forms a legacy from which contemporary nurses have arguably yet to break free. Resonances between the past and the present can be detected in contemporary discussions of the 'presentation' of the nurse, which bring the characteristics, manner and emotional display of the nurse into sharper focus (Ersser, 1991). Such concerns would seem to militate against any unqualified claims of 'progress' in nursing. Indeed, it can be argued that the emphasis of the so-called 'new nursing' on individualism, humanistic psychology and the personal characteristics of the nurse, echoes the essentialist arguments of an earlier period and debate.

POINTS FOR DISCUSSION

The overwhelming response to Rafferty's paper was one of depression at how little things had changed in nursing! By all accounts, the same tensions as outlined by Rafferty were still influencing the way nursing was being interpreted and executed. The tension between the hospital medical model of care and the more community-based social hygiene model of intervention which originated in the mid-19th century was continuing to cause problems for nurses in the 1990s. Similarly, the debate between whether nursing was primarily an art and a calling rather than a science requiring a sound intellectual grasp of a range of technologies continues to exercise the minds and prejudices of the profession. And perhaps most interestingly, the tension between woman's role as subordinated moral agent, ministering to the physical, spiritual and emotional needs of mankind, as opposed to the image of woman as independent, autonomous professional, working in partnership with medical colleagues, continues to cause confusion. This tension is important to understand as it affects – and has significantly influenced – a range of decisions about the contribution nursing has been allowed to make and will make to society.

The discussion centred around three key areas where the above tensions seemed to have paralysed any real progress in nursing. These were educational reforms in nursing, the self-image of both the profession and nurses, and finally the vision nursing had for the future.

On the question of education, opinions moved in two rather opposite directions. One was related to the fascination that debates regarding the supervision, examination and registration of nurses were still considering the same points as were first identified in the late 1800s. This was seen to reflect the complexity of the task of training nurses and the still unresolved question as to how one teaches another person to be a safe, competent carer. Less optimistically, there was a view that because nursing worked in a culture which consistently undervalued the nurturing, caring skills that nurses bring to the workplace, no educational system will do proper justice to the clear explanation of such skills and attributes. In a curious way it was thought that Nightingale's determination to keep nursing education located in the everyday experiences of practical caring, guided by trusted 'moral tutors', was one way of protecting these very attributes.

The general despondency of the group following Rafferty's presentation was interpreted by some as an illustration of nursing's confusion about its own identity. The role as developed by western society has carried within it so many paradoxes and tensions that these work against nurses joining together to move more confidently toward achieving certain objectives. This lack of conceptual clarity was discussed in an earlier paper by Kitson, and yet Rafferty's work shows that almost from the beginning of the development of modern nursing there has been a division in the way people want to think about nursing.

The vexed question of why nursing cannot change itself or achieve certain changes in education, management, work practices and so on, was beginning to become clearer. Perhaps to summarize the shared feeling of the group as realizing they were hostages to past tensions would not clearly reflect their desire to be more determined to change things for the future.

REFERENCES

Abel-Smith, B. (1960) *A History of the Nursing Profession*, London, Heinemann.
Abel-Smith, B. (1964) *The Hospitals*, London, Heinemann, pp. 43–45.
Baly, M. (1984) *The Influence of the Nightingale Fund from 1855–1914 on the Development of Nursing*. PhD Thesis, University of London, p.260.
Baly, M. (1986) *Florence Nightingale and the Nursing Legacy*, London, Croom Helm, pp. 230–232.
Barwell, R. (1857) *The Care of the Sick: a Course of Practical Lectures Delivered at the Working Women's College London*, London, Chapman and Hall, p. 101.
Benton, S. (1877) *Nurses and Nursing*, London, Henry Kimpton p. 6.
Bonham-Carter, H. (1892) *Memorandum on the Registration of Nurses and the Royal British Nurses Association in Memorandum against the Petition*, London.
Breay, M. and Fenwick, E. (1928) History of the International Council of Nurses 1899–1909. *International Council of Nurses Annual Reports* 1928–29, pp. 215–275.
Burdett Papers (1909) Central Hospitals Council for London, Box A1(2) *State Registration of Nurses*, Bodleian Library, Oxford.
Burstyn, J. (1983) *Victorian Education and the Ideal of Womanhood*, London, Croom Helm.
Davin, A. (1978) Imperialism and motherhood. *History Workshop* 5, 9–66.
Digby, A. (1978) *Pauper Palaces: Studies in Economic History*, London, Routledge and Kegan Paul, pp. 189–196.

Dingwall, R., Rafferty, A. M., and Webster, C. (1988) *An Introduction to the Social History of Nursing*, Routledge London, pp. 77–97.

Dock, L. (1905) State Registration. *British Journal of Nursing* **34**, 149.

Ersser, S. (1991) A search for the therapeutic dimension of nurse–patient interaction, in *Nursing as Therapy*, (eds R. McMahon and A. Pearson), London, Chapman and Hall, pp. 43–84.

Eyler, J. (1979) *Victorian Social Medicine and the Ideas and Methods of William Farr*, Baltimore, Johns Hopkins University Press.

Fenwick, Mrs B. (1890) Evidence to the Select Committee of the House of Lords on Metropolitan Hospitals. *Parliamentary Papers* **XVI.I**, HMSO, p. 554.

Fenwick, Mrs B. (1892) Evidence to the Select Committee of the House of Lords on Metropolitan Hospitals. *Parliamentary Papers* **XII.I**, HMSO, pp. 452, 455, 554, 555.

Gamarnikov, E. (1991) Nurse or Woman: Gender and Professionalism in Reformed Nursing 1860-1923, in *Anthropology and Nursing* (eds P. Holden and J. Littlewood), London, Routledge pp. 110–129.

Hall, C. (1979) The early formation of Victorian domestic ideology, in *Fit Work for Women*, (ed. S. Burman), London, Croom Helm, pp. 15–32.

Hogg, S. (1967) *Nursing History: the State of the Art*, London, pp. 176–189.

Holden, P. and Littlewood, J. (eds) (1991) *Anthropology and Nursing*, London, pp. 110–129.

Holland, S. (1904) House of Commons Select Committee on Registration of Nurses, London, HMSO, p. 55.

Lewis, J. (1980) *The Politics of Motherhood*, London, Croom Helm.

Maggs, C. (1987) Profit and loss and the hospital nurse, in *Nursing History: the State of the Art* (ed. S. Hogg), London, Croom Helm, pp. 176–189.

Nightingale, F. (1883) *Notes on Hospitals*, London, Longmans, Green, p. 18.

Nightingale, F. (1894) Sick nursing and health nursing, in *Hospitals, Dispensaries and Nursing: Papers and Discussions at the International Congress of Charities, Correction and Philanthropy, Section III*, Chicago, June 12–17, 1893, Baltimore, London, Scientific Press, p. 444.

Peterson, M.J. (1978) *The Medical Profession in Mid-Victorian England*, Berkeley, University of California Press, reprinted by Virago, pp. 14–15.

Pinchbeck, I. (1985) *Women Workers and the Industrial Revolution 1750–1850*, London, pp. 194–201.

Purvis, J. (1981) 'Women's life is essentially domestic, public life being confined to men' (Comte): Separate spheres and inequality in the education of working class women 1854–1900. *History of Education* **10**, 227–243.

Quain, R. (ed.) (1882) *Dictionary of Medicine*, London, Longmans, Green, p. 1043.

Rafferty, A. M. (1989) Some historical aspects of the International Council of Nurses, in *Nursing in the World*, (eds K. Robinson, A. M. Rafferty, G. Bergman, L. Quam and J. Quinlan), Distance Learning Centre at the Polytechnic of the Southbank, London, pp. A11–A12.

Rathbone, W. (1892) Evidence to the Select Committee of the House of Lords on Metropolitan Hospitals. *Parliamentary Papers* **XIII.I**, HMSO, p. xci.

Reverby, S. (1987) *Ordered to Care: the Dilemma of American Nursing 1850-1945*, Cambridge, CUP, pp. 60–75.

Robinson, K. and Rafferty, A. M. (1988) *Nursing Workforce*, London, Distance Learning Centre at the Polytechnic of the Southbank, pp. 30–38.

Rosenberg, C. (1979) Florence Nightingale and contagion: the hospital as a moral universe, in *Healing and History: Essays for George Rosen*, (ed. C. Rosenberg), New York, Science History Publications, pp. 116–136.

Rosenberg, C. (1987) *The Care of Strangers: the Rise of America's Hospital System*, New York, Basic Books, pp. 166–189, 212–236.

Summers, A. (1988) *Angels and Citizens: British Women as Military Nurses 1854–1914*, London, Routledge, p. 21.
Trudgill, E. (1976) *Madonnas and Magdalens*, London, Heinemann.
Williams, K. (1980) From Sarah Gamp to Florence Nightingale, in *Rewriting Nursing History*, (ed C. Davies), London, Croom Helm, pp. 41–75.

5

A cross-cultural perspective on nursing in Europe

Agnes Bjorn

5.1 INTRODUCTION

A study on transcultural care can focus on diversity – how nursing care is provided differently in east, west, north and south, according to culture, resources, political decisions and geography. In the European region of the World Health Organisation (WHO) there are 32 countries and the nursing care provided is certainly different. This paper will, however, focus as much on universalities and similarities, developments during the last decade in nursing in Europe, as on the differences. In particular it will describe the development of a number of key collaborative projects which have enabled nurses in European countries to get together to discuss their work. These include the WHO/European Programme, the setting up of the work group of European Nurse Researchers in 1978, and an outline of some of the more recent WHO developments in nursing, including primary health care, quality assurance, leadership and nursing diagnosis.

5.2 PEOPLE'S NEED FOR NURSING CARE PROJECT

This study contributed to the WHO/European General Programme 1980 by:

1. Helping to disseminate existing knowledge by identifying innovative and improved health care approaches in member states;
2. Promoting priority research;
3. Acting as a catalyst in promoting national health policy development towards the aim of 'Health for All by the Year 2000';
4. Improving cooperation and coordination between international organizations active in the health field.

An underlying tenet for WHO in promoting innovative and improved health care was to support a primary health care approach. This is based essentially on equity in health, i.e., that health care should not just be provided according to demand. Rather, it should be planned according to the needs of the population with the aim of health promotion. The strategy 'Health for All by Year 2000' is based on primary health care which supports the following principles:

1.   Health care should be related to the needs of the population;
2.   Consumers should participate, individually and collectively in the planning and implementation of health care;
3.   Fullest use must be made of available resources;
4.   Primary health care is not an isolated approach but the most local part of a comprehensive system.

While this was an overarching policy promoted by WHO and discussed by health care professionals in numerous countries, the actual study 'People's needs for nursing care' aimed to focus the debate on to what was actually happening to nursing in various countries, and how research areas were being identified.

The study did act as a catalyst in promoting nursing research and drawing attention to the nursing contribution both within the profession (nurses gained a better understanding of their professional work and how innovations could develop through research) and outside the profession, where other health workers began to see nursing research not as a threat but rather as complementary to innovation in health care.

The last goal, of improving cooperation and coordination between international organizations active in the health field, was seen as very important by the then Regional Nursing Officer, Dr Dorothy Hall. She found that it was time for nurses to begin to get to know each other and learn from one another. Nurses, she believed, should be able to gather at international conferences and call on each other to sort out professional matters – in other words, to identify themselves as a professional group.

This happened during the late 1970s, when we in Europe were about to have EEC directives for professional registration and nurses in several countries of the EEC were afraid that if they had to conform to other countries' requirements it would mean a lowering of the quality of their education and consequently of their standards of care. Dorothy Hall wanted to strengthen the nursing profession, and emphasized that nurses could learn something from each other, or even better, that nurses could work together for general improvements in the standard of care.

The cross-national nursing study on 'People's Needs for Nursing Care' was launched in 1980. Nurses in 10 European countries participated and 23 participating centres were established. Nine different languages were spoken. The official language was English although it was for most participants their second, third or fourth language. Some meetings were conducted bilingually if the host country would finance it.

At national level a programme manager was responsible for teaching the nurses in the participating centre and implementing the study (using local language) as decided by the group of programme managers. The preparation for the study took approximately two years and the implementation another two years. Data collection instruments (a health assessment form and a nursing care plan), coding and data processing protocols were developed and used. Many examples of the spin-offs from these exercises can be given. One example is the definition of terms we were forced to come to an agreement on, which were translated into nine working languages and have since been widely used in most countries. Another example is from the discussion on the nursing process where each programme manager presented their view. The Czechoslovakian nurse representative explained that she had no access to international literature, and therefore was not familiar with the literature on the nursing process. However, in her doctoral study she had tried to develop a model for a nursing approach which she called 'active nursing', where the emphasis was on the interaction between the nurse and client, and the realization that the nurse can act independently in providing care. The independent action by the nurse was important for her to emphasize, whereas others might see it as a fault. But should we not learn from her and be more aware of developing independent nursing interventions? At least her description of active nursing showed that it did comply with the nursing process. Thus, as is recognized in other professions, similar theories are developing simultaneously in different places.

The results of the study were more the outcome of the process (professional development) than scientific results. Before the study began it was political reasoning which decided that nursing in different countries should not be compared. As we worked through the analysis process it was, however, clear that it was rather misleading to report only on the aggregated data. Some differences by centres could not be overlooked. For example, as shown in Figure 5.1, the results of documentation of objectives for care and nursing interventions differed less by sample group than by centre. In fact, there were rather small differences between the two sample groups in the same centre. The differences by centre were due to differences in education and culture as well as health service provision.

The conclusions and recommendations of the study were fed back to the WHO General Programme, and the recommendations in particular emphasize what was achieved in this study and what still needed to be done in order for nursing to contribute to the WHO's programme for Health for All by Year 2000. For example, it was possible for nurses to develop a tool for the holistic and systematic recording of needs for nursing care, and also to document the care in a nursing care plan. The tools should be further developed for wider use. The data processing tools should also be further developed and used to establish information systems for documenting nursing care.

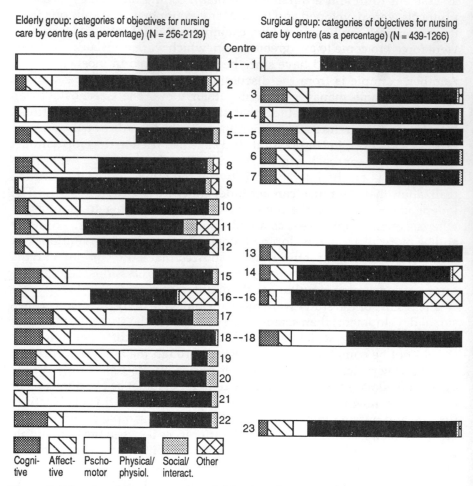

Elderly group: categories of objectives for nursing care by centre (as a percentage) (N = 256-2129)

Surgical group: categories of objectives for nursing care by centre (as a percentage) (N = 439-1266)

Centre

Cogni- Affect- Pscho- Physical/ Social/ Other
tive   tive   motor   physiol. interact.

Figure 5.1 Results of documentation of objectives for care and nursing interventions showing differences by centres

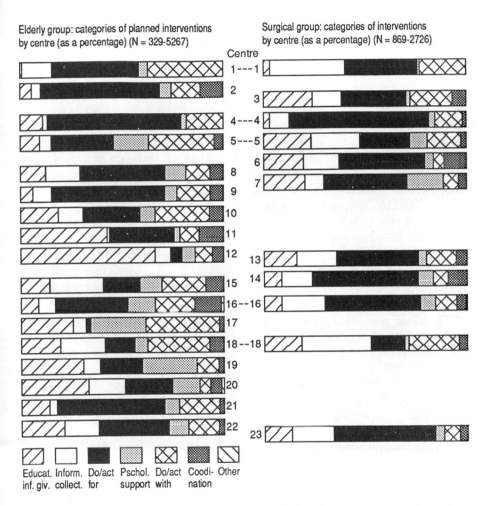

Figure 5.1 *(cont.)* Results of documentation of objectives for care and nursing interventions showing differences by centres.

5.3 ESTABLISHING THE WORKGROUP OF EUROPEAN NURSE RESEARCHERS (WENR)

Another issue in the European developments in nursing which took place in the same decade was the establishment of the Workgroup of European Nurse Researchers (WENR). This was also inspired and encouraged by Dr Hall, who stated that nurses needed a professional forum. More directly, it was the consequence of a discussion about cooperation in research during the International Council of Nurses (ICN) congress in Tokyo in 1977, and a subsequent resolution was passed to arrange a conference for nurse researchers within Europe.

A Dutch nurse, Haneke van Manen, called the first meeting in 1978, inviting nurse researchers from the European nursing associations in membership with the ICN. The basic idea was that research is necessary for the development of a sound knowledge base for nursing practice, and that nursing would benefit from closer contact through promotion or research. A conference would present an opportunity to collect, present and discuss information regarding the state of nursing research within Europe, and to explore the conditions for the development and promotion of nursing research.

The WENR is an independent workgroup with representation from the European nursing associations in memberships with the ICN. It has no budget and no permanent address. Meetings are organized by a steering committee and members attend on behalf of their nursing association at the expense of that association.

The close relationship with nursing associations in membership with the ICN has limited representation in some countries. In the Nordic countries most nurses are members of their national association: in Denmark, 95–97% of active nurses are members. In the UK approximately 65% of nurses are members of the Royal College of Nursing. However, in France there are approximately 60 associations and one of the smaller groups is in membership of the ICN. The majority of nurses in France are members of a Catholic national and international association which does not have official ICN recognition. In Belgium there are Catholic, Protestant, Francophone and Flemish associations. In Yugoslavia there is an association in each province, but they send representatives in turn. It should be mentioned that most countries have tried to send a representative to WENR.

WENR has met annually since 1978. Nursing associations have in turn hosted WENR and publicized proceedings of the meetings. Every other year the meeting is extended with an international (European) open conference. These meetings have provided the richest information on nursing care, education and research in Europe. This is reflected in the number of abstracts, papers and participants in the open conferences (Table 5.1).

In the very early stages it was seen as important that high-quality research papers were presented, but also that countries where nursing re-

Table 5.1 Abstracts, papers and participants in the Open Conferences (approximate numbers)

Year & Host	Submitted Abstracts	Accepted Abstracts	Participants	Countries
1982 Sweden	70	50	350	26
1984 England	150	80	600	27
1986 Finland	120	93	300	24
1988 Israel	140	105	250	29

search was at its embryo stage were also represented. Ironically, the paper which received the most attention from the press in the first Open Conference at Uppsala was presented by an inexperienced researcher. However, it was a topical issue and it was presented in a 'lay' manner, which appealed to the press. Experienced researchers could learn from that!

The European nursing field is different today compared to the late 1970s. Changes have taken place in higher education in nursing, new degree courses have been established and conditions for carrying out nursing research have improved in many countries.

5.4 NURSING IN EUROPE TODAY: WHO DEVELOPMENTS

Other important activities have also taken place. The WHO/European Nursing Unit has had a turnover of staff and other task-force groups have been formed. For example, a major programme in nursing quality assurance and standards was created in 1982 which spearheaded the dissemination of information of this topic throughout Europe. Other task forces were set up on topics such as leadership in nursing; prevention of family breakdown with particular focus on the consequences for children; and the determination of the spread of AIDS. The task forces are always defined within the overall framework of the WHO programme, namely the strategy on HFA 2000.

5.5 PRIMARY HEALTH CARE

Influenced by the WHO strategy, the common issue for development in nursing is a primary health care approach in some countries. In England, for example, it might be called a community approach, but it has commonalities with the WHO target programme HFA 2000. The emphasis on primary health care is reflected in care planning, education, priority research and conference themes. The most influential conference was organized by WHO/Europe, with invited representatives from the 32 European countries. It had approximately 200 participants, with 109 presentations, all related to primary health care. Most importantly, recommendations and resolutions on the nursing contribution to HFA 2000 in implementing primary health care were given.

The primary health care approach is an emphasis that the western world may have learned, or may have to learn from the non-western world. Leininger, a well known American researcher in cross-cultural nursing, identifies some major contrasts between western and non-western world views that merit consideration to understand both qualitative and quantitative methods of research. She states such differences between western and non-western as being related to variations in philosophical, historical, religious, cultural and social ideologies, and process through time. In my view some of these differences could also reflect the differences between research in a primary health care approach and research in a hospital care approach, as shown in Table 5.2.

When I analysed Leininger's scheme, I began to understand why I could not get the North American nurses to accept that the NANDA Nursing Diagnosis was lacking in environmental and psychosocial issues: these issues may not be important within their philosophy. Through collaboration with colleagues from eastern Europe, I have learned how they integrate their environment into health care planning and how they accept that planning in nursing is dependent on political decisions – hence they are, or they have to be, part of the political decision making process.

5.6 LEADERSHIP IN HEALTH CARE

The Director General of WHO, Dr Mahler, stated in 1986 that leadership is critical to narrow the gap between policy and action: 'Leaders lead, and leadership is characterized by visionary inspiration which shapes the very values of society'. If nurses want to take on leadership within health care and play an important role in health services they must be able to demonstrate what their contribution will be. Therefore, they need to formulate a community nursing framework and clarify nursing terminology. Thus the population will know exactly what kind of health services can be provided by nurses. In the political context, nurses need to be able to demonstrate the contribution they can make to the improvement of the health of the population.

'If you have a plan you can act, if you do not have a plan you can only react', said Dr Marie Farrell, Regional Officer for Nursing in WHO/Europe 1982–89. This way of thinking has dominated the nursing unit of WHO/Europe and I would query that, but I would like to say that it also dominates the nursing profession in Europe.

In order to assess and plan future health services, it is necessary to collect and accumulate information about the population's health status to support what is already available in the official health statistics. In other words, to develop a health and nursing epidemiology. I find that it is necessary for nurses in Europe to continue to get together and work on these issues.

Table 5.2 Contrasts between western and non-western philosophical world view influencing research paradigms. Western orientation tends to comply with a hospital approach, while non-western orientation tends to comply with a primary health care approach

Western orientation	*Non-western orientation*
Focus is on recent human conditions, events, and future developments.	Focus is on early and prehistorical human conditions or events.
Emphasis is on biological, chemical, economical, technological, psychological, and genetic factors to explain human behaviour, especially rational thinking modes.	Emphasis is on philosophical, historical, epistemological, and esthetical explanations about human behaviour. Deal with rational and irrational thought.
Use an action and testing focus to 'prove' reality and causes.	Use a contemplative and reflective focus to know and understand reality or nonreality.
Use logical deductions and systematized database to study and explain phenomena.	Use humanistic, cultural, social, experiential, philosophical, historical, and a variety of other means to know and explain circumstances.
Focus is primarily on individuals and small groups who are to be studied and explained.	Focus is on families, institutions, corporate groups, history, civilizations, and humanistic experiences which are to be explained and understood.
Humans are complex, but can be known by a few significant variables of a biophysical, emotional, economical and social nature. Reduction to uni-causes or a few variables prevails.	Human behaviour is complex and multifaceted, but it is human conditions, lifeways, and quality of life through time that are important with religion, culture, values, and history providing *multiexplanatory* findings.
Research largely focused on objective reality to verify phenomena (extrinsic factors important).	Research focused on both subjective and objective factors to know the situation or condition (intrinsic factors slightly more important than extrinsic ones).
Focus on discrete human behaviour, problem solving, and proving reality by testing.	Focus on human conditions, symbols, rituals, lifeways, and patterns are important.
Emphasis on experimental and quasi-experimental (measurable) research.	Emphasis on naturalistic (environmentalist) research.
Holds that reality experiences are objective and definable.	Focus on spiritualism, magic, healing potential, aestheticism and mysticism to be understood.
Time and changes are very imortant (now and in the near future).	Changes within cultural values and within historical, contextual, and environmental factors are important, especially past historical factors.
Totality of life experiences is important (the 'wholistic perspective').	Parts, objects, and selected aspects of life are important.(the 'piece-perspective').
Objects, things, and relationships are of prime importance.	Context, people, and historical situations are the most important.
Focus on individuals' health problems.	Focus on health needs of the individual, groups and populations.
Care and cure for individuals.	
Prioritize technology.	Prioritize environment and lifestyle conducive to health.
Demography and epidemiological trends.	

It is time to consider whether alternative or complementary ways of cooperation and communication should be explored. I suggest that nurses in Europe get together like nurses in North America, and work out their strategy and set up consortia for the development of professional issues.

POINTS FOR DISCUSSION

Agnes Bjorn's paper attempts to move beyond the debates over the conceptual derivation of skills and knowledge within nursing and caring, to a more descriptive account of similarities and differences in practice that may exist in Europe. Of interest was the central role played by WHO (Europe) in facilitating nursing dialogue across Europe. Throughout descriptions of a number of key programmes, Bjorn outlines the sometimes painful pathway to ensure effective dialogue between colleagues. It is noteworthy that until WHO's involvement, little opportunity existed for nurses to share ideas or discuss issues related to nursing policy, practice or education. The fact that some European countries still do not appreciate the need for nurses to come together to discuss health care matters is a reflection of past societal attitudes towards nursing and caring, and present health care systems that continue to disenfranchise the voice of nursing.

The debate following Bjorn's paper centred around three main areas, namely nurses and politics, the relationship between the UK and WHO, and some discussion on how new areas for nursing development were identified within a European context.

There was unanimous agreement that nurses should be more politically astute in terms of knowing how to introduce issues of concern into national and international agendas. The (relative) lack of success of nursing in influencing health policy in organizations such as WHO was seen to be related to the lack of any local activities involving nurses. The argument was put forward that if major change was to occur at a national level, then nurses had to be more committed to campaigning for change at local level. The role of the professional organization was also identified as being important in furthering the debate on health policy issues. Examples of effective professional networks were given, and questions were raised as to how government and professional organizations can best work together to improve communication.

An interesting debate emerged regarding the UK's attitude towards the role and function of WHO Europe. Many participants admitted to knowing little about the programmes or activities of WHO, although on hearing what was happening they agreed that it was particularly useful. Ways of improving communication between government and professional representatives of WHO working parties and the rest of the profession were discussed, some quite imaginative solutions being presented. A very obvious omission was the failure of the profession to circulate WHO literature on a wider scale.

The importance of nurses being involved in wider health care policy debates, both nationally and on a European level, was highlighted again when the discussion turned to considering how new areas for nursing development were determined. Obvious patterns within health care were influencing nursing priorities. The paradox, however, still remained, which was, given the central part nurses play in health care delivery, why is it that they continue to play such a subordinate role when it comes to identifying health policy and research priorities and the allocation of funds?

FURTHER READING

Ashworth, P. *et al.* (1987) *People's Needs for Nursing Care, A European Study*, World Health Organisation, Copenhagen.

Christensen, E. H. and Lerheim, K. (1990) Proceedings of the 10th Workgroup meeting, Portugal 1987 and the 11th Workgroup meeting, 4th Open Conference Israel 1988. WENR, Copenhagen.

Dorfmeister, A. *et al.* (eds) (1986) *Pflegeforschung für eine bessere Krankenpflege,* Proceedings of the 8th Workgroup meeting. WENR, Vienna.

Leininger, M. M. (1984) *Qualitative Research Methods in Nursing,* W. B. Saunders Company.

Maglacas, A. (1988) European Strategy. Nursing in the Fast Lane. *Nursing Standard,* July 2, pp. 8–9.

Mahler, H. (1986) *Why leadership for health for all?* Keynote address, 7 April 1986, Leadership in Nursing for Health for All, Tokyo, Japan.

Stinson, S. M; Kerr, J. C. (eds) (1986) *International Issues in Nursing Research,* Croom Helm, The Charles Press.

World Health Organisation (1985) Targets for health for all: Targets in support of the European regional stragegy for health for all. WHO/EURO, Copenhagen.

World Health Organisation (1988) Summary Report, European Conference on Nursing, Vienna, 21–24 June 1988, EUR/HAF Target 27. WHO, Copenhagen.

6

Problems with paradigms in a caring profession

Jane Robinson

'... clearing intellectual jungles is also a respectable occupation. Perhaps every science must start with metaphor and end with algebra; and perhaps without the metaphor there would never have been any algebra.'

Max Black (1962)

6.1 INTRODUCTION

The nature of nursing knowledge and its relationship to practice were issues which concerned me greatly when I first embarked on research during the 1970s. Indeed, Chapter 2 of *An Evaluation of Health Visiting* (Robinson, 1982) which is entitled 'Theoretical perspectives affecting the development of health visiting practice', concluded that:

> '... the absence of any critical evaluation of the ways in which the different theoretical perspectives taught during ... training have influenced subsequent practice may have contributed to the role conflicts experienced by health visitors. The situation may have been exacerbated firstly by the assumption that integration of knowledge is both desirable and feasible, and secondly by the differing expectations of the health visitor held by various members of her role set.
>
> It has been suggested that the health visitor may attempt to resolve the conflict inherent in certain situations by moving towards either a clinical or a social science perspective. Further exploration of this proposition would appear to be essential.'

Hopefully this statement establishes my personal credentials as a nurse who has long been deeply concerned with the relationship of knowledge to practice, as this paper embarks on a rather critical evaluation of some of nursing's more extreme claims to scientific knowledge. Colours should be nailed to the mast immediately and an admission made of disquiet

arising from some of the more extreme debates over the untested, hypo-
thetical, highly abstract models of nursing which were taking place between 1985 and 1988. At the time, when I was acting as a temporary
adviser to the World Health Organisation European Region on the content
and organization of a Conference on Nursing (held in Vienna in June
1988), a consultant joined us who had numerous models of nursing at her
fingertips,and these she exhorted us to adopt for European nursing practice (Robinson, 1987). A tiny minority of these models did originate from
Europe, but the vast majority emanated from North America where, as far
as one was able to ascertain, they had rarely been tested empirically in the
practice situation. (The term 'empirical' denotes that '... the propositions
of social science must be tested against observational data to survive as
tenable generalizations...' (Bulmer, 1982)) It hardly needs pointing out
how very different from Europe or the United Kingdom the health care
culture is where the majority of the models had been developed. This call
to general application without rigorous evaluation appeared therefore to
be, at best, poor science; at worst it appeared to epitomize aspects of
intellectual imperialism.

This is not to deny that a 'longing for a regular pattern into which
the whole of human experience can be fitted' may be an extremely
common phenomenon (Robinson, 1982). Olive Stevenson has suggested
that this longing for regularity in patterns of thinking is widespread.
However, in the context of social work, she rejected the idea of a 'body
of knowledge' as a prerequisite for social work's claim to professionalism, saying:

> 'To me ... this phrase conveys an idea of something too static, too
> formed, to be possible or desirable in the present state of the social
> sciences and social work. It is vitally important that we should not be
> talking at this stage in our development as if the knowledge upon which
> we can draw had a shape and clear cut boundaries ...'
>
> (Stevenson, 1974)

Instead, she developed the notion of 'frames of reference' which

> '... may complement or conflict. There is a pressing need to analyse
> these issues further and until this is done we will do little to help our
> students with the task of synthesis for practice which must be our
> ultimate objective. There must, for example, be rigorous comparative
> study of different approaches to the understanding of human behavi-
> our so that we may see more clearly where there is genuine conflict,
> where merely semantic difficulties.'
>
> (Stevenson, 1974)

There is much to commend this modest approach to the elucidation and
generation of knowledge for practice to nursing, lest we all try to claim
too much and end up looking ridiculous in the process. We shall be better

academics if we recognize the multiple sources of knowledge on which we draw. Although we may apply *natural* science knowledge in some aspects of nursing practice (and therefore need to understand the different frames of reference to which natural science relates), we have also to distinguish between this knowledge and knowledge for the activities which we call 'nursing', and which in themselves represent a *social* process. This process has to be analysed with the tools which help us to better clarify and develop the concepts which increase our understanding of what we call 'nursing' within it. This aspect of nursing knowledge will be returned to later but, for the present, let us turn to 'Paradigms and Problems of a Caring Profession' which was the title originally given for this paper. Although the title is interesting it is not clear what was intended in the context of nursing knowledge. It will be necessary therefore to construct what one believes may have been intended. This construction will attempt to show that, by using ambiguous and rather pretentious terms, nursing obscures rather than clarifies the conceptual foundations of its knowledge base. In carrying out this analysis it has become clear that the title as given was inappropriate. I have therefore presumed to alter it slightly but perhaps significantly to 'Problems with paradigms in a caring profession'.

6.2 FORMS OF KNOWLEDGE: CLEARING THE UNDERGROWTH

It is assumed that the term 'paradigm' refers loosely to Thomas Kuhn's usage in *The Structure of Scientific Revolutions* (Kuhn, 1962, 1970). Unfortunately, instead of helping, this focus reveals several problems relating to rigour and appropriateness, which will be addressed in turn. First, Kuhn was a physicist who stumbled accidentally into the history of ideas surrounding his subject more than 10 years before he published the first edition of his account of scientific revolutions in 1962. The impact of this book was undoubtedly startling. Regis (1987) asserts, for example, that:

> '... by 1969 Kuhn was one of the two or three most frequently cited authors in the United States. People suddenly began to see "paradigms" and "paradigm shifts" everywhere – almost as if it were a sport, an egghead recreation of some kind – and for a while your adroitness in juggling paradigmatic shifts and cosmic revolutions became an index of your metascientific enlightenment and degree of intellectual chic.'
>
> (Regis, 1987)

Yet Kuhn's starting point was the study of the revolutionary phases in the development of physics. Central to his differentiation of the natural sciences was the idea of a 'paradigm'. On the one hand, he argues, lie 'mature' sciences with clearly established paradigms; on the other are those whose development is still at a pre-paradigmatic stage. Kuhn (1970) claims that the ability of key theorists

'... implicitly to define the legitimate problems and methods of a re-search field for succeeding generations of practitioners [lay in] two essential characteristics. Their achievement was sufficiently unprece-dented to attract an enduring group of adherents away from competing modes of scientific activity. Simultaneously, it was sufficiently open-ended to leave all sorts of problems for the redefined group of practi-tioners to resolve.'

(Kuhn, 1970)

He continues:

'Achievements that share these two characteristics I shall henceforth refer to as "paradigms", a term that relates closely to "normal science". By choosing it, I mean to suggest that some accepted examples of actual scientific practice – examples which include law, theory, application and instrumentation together – provide *models* (my emphasis) from which spring particular coherent traditions of scientific research.'

(Kuhn, 1970)

Kuhn asserts quite emphatically that an open question remains as to what parts of social science have yet acquired such paradigms at all. Here is the first problem: a major obstacle to the use of the term 'paradigm' in relation to nursing knowledge exists because, if the term is used as Kuhn describes it above, it can be seen to be quite inappropriate for nursing, which is neither 'mature' nor 'normal' science.

An example of the imprecision which results from non-rigorous use of the terminology is shown in an article by Eriksson (1989) entitled 'Caring Paradigms'. Citing a Swedish author, Törnebohm, (1985), she claims that the paradigm consists of four components:

1. The interests of the researcher/practitioner that describes what she *wants* to do.
2. The competence of the researcher/practitioner sets that limits what she is *able* to do [sic].
3. The world view of the researcher/practitioner consisting of a number of general assumptions about that part of reality in which she acts.
4. The view of science which includes a comprehension of the develop-ment of the caring discipline, the present state of the research field, how the actual science is related to other sciences, what kind of issues the researchers in the field deal with, how they work, how the science is related to its territory and prospects of the development of the science in the future.

It is not necessary to lay claim to membership of a 'mature' or 'normal' scientific community in order to assert that this global view of nursing's world order is unlikely to lead to acceptable scholarship, but also that it will not facilitate the relationship of knowledge to practice.

The second problem with any attempt to extrapolate Kuhn's notion of paradigms to nursing lies in the critical distinction which has been made between the forms of knowledge with which we are concerned. Becher (1989), a philosopher, carried out ethnographic research in order to map 'The variegated territory of academic knowledge' and to explore 'the diverse characteristics of those who inhabit and cultivate it'. In a fascinating study of 220 academics in 12 different academic disciplines, Becher develops a taxonomy which applies to their knowledge forms and knowledge communities. The taxonomy includes distinctions between:

1. Restricted/unrestricted knowledge
2. Hard/soft knowledge
3. Convergent/divergent communities
4. Pure/applied disciplines.

Physics emerges to the extreme left of the spectrum on all four dimensions. It is quantitative, has a well developed theoretical structure embracing causal propositions, generalizable findings and universal laws. Its community sense is convergent with a strong sense of commonality,

'collective kinship, a mutuality of interests, a shared intellectual style, a consensual understanding of "profound simplicities", and even "a quasi-religious belief in the unity of nature". It is not easy to doubt that physicists share a particular way of approaching problems, a collective ideology and even a common world view.'

(Becher, 1989)

It is not difficult to imagine from this analysis that any new developments which shook physicists' commonly held world view would indeed constitute a 'revolution' in the Kuhnian sense of the word. To suggest that a similar perception may be held of nursing knowledge is frankly ludicrous for it has almost exactly opposite characteristics:

'... unclear boundaries, problems which are broad in scope but loose in definition, a relatively unspecific theoretical structure, a concern with the qualitative and particular, and a reiterative pattern of enquiry.'

(Becher, 1989)

Nurses resemble far more the geographers and pharmacists in Becher's study, being:

'highly multidisciplinary, having numerous overlaps with neighbouring subject groups and a heterogeneous set of professional concerns. Papers in these two fields frequently appear in the journals of other disciplines, with the result that the journals dedicated to their own disciplines tend to be weakly supported and lacking in prestige.'

(Becher, 1989)

Nursing knowledge, furthermore, is like pharmacy in Becher's study – highly applied. Nursing's uncritical tendency to appropriate the methods and language of what it believes to be 'science' in an apparent attempt to appear 'scientific' without attempting to consider some of the related philosophical problems is a matter of major concern. The term 'paradigm' does not, of course, appear too often in the nursing literature, but its synonym, 'model', in the sense of a pattern or exemplar, does. In 1985, when I began to think a great deal about some nurses' claims to a unique 'nursing science', the literature was searched for a lead on a philosophy of science perspective on models. The search was not particularly fruitful although one text, Black's (1962) critique of the ways in which the term 'models' is used without rigour in natural scientific discourse, confirmed that imprecision abounds. If the critique is applicable to natural science, it is even more appropriate for nursing. Consider this introduction by McFarlane (1986) to the nature of nursing models:

> '... A great deal of the literature dealing with models is confusing, largely because the terminology is used inconsistently and the language is convoluted .... As I write I have a number of models around me – an inkstand with a model of a 1918 field ambulance on it, a doll dressed as a Welsh lady, a platypus .... A real black cat competes for space, but he is a cat; the model is a representation of him, as are all the other models representations only of the reality that they represent.
>
> Models of nursing, then, are representations of the reality of nursing practice. They represent the factors at work and how they are related.' (Kershaw and Salvage, 1986).

> (McFarlane, 1986)

Here is an example of what Black describes as the metaphorical – a descriptive term being transferred to some object to which it is not properly applicable. McFarlane here is mistakenly equating nursing models (whatever they may be) with models in the literal sense. That is, a three-dimensional miniature, 'more or less true to scale' (Black, 1962). Nurses may indeed use scale models, such as those of the heart or kidney, in order to learn about the structure and function of the human body, but these are emphatically *not* nursing models in the sense that McFarlane describes them.

Black goes on to discuss three further, distinct types of model. The second, a type of design, something worthy of imitation – a model husband, model Ford or fashion model – is mentioned but then dismissed as irrelevant in Black's discussion. He then compares scale and analogue models, both of which are symbolic representations of some real or imaginary original. Scale models, however, rely upon visual identity. Analogue models, by contrast, are guided by the more abstract aim of reproducing the *structure* of the original, inasmuch that there is a point by point correspondence between the model's pattern of relationships and the original. Black cites hydraulic models of economic systems or the use of electrical circuits in computers as examples of analogue models. It is possible that nurses may use diagrams in their discussion of nursing models in the mistaken belief that they represent an analogue model. These diagrams may illustrate a hypothesized abstract relationship between certain elements in a health care system. Diagrams may play a useful role in helping nurses (especially novices) to conceptualize, say, the relationship between nursing, the person, the environment and health (overlapping circles are popular) but they are emphatically *not* analogue models – they are diagrams.

Mathematical models, Black's fourth example, involve the identification and mathematical manipulation of a number of relevant variables, either selected on the basis of common sense or derived from theoretical considerations. The models of nursing labour supply and wastage, or of a country's population growth, depending on certain assumptions – for example, about birth and death rates – are instances of mathematical models. There are inevitable drawbacks when they are applied – as nursing supply modelling illustrates – as the drastic simplification of a complex social reality can result in a risk of confusing the accuracy of the mathematics with the strength of empirical verification in the field. Nor can mathematics provide any causal explanation for the phenomena described; strength of association between two or more variables is the limit of the explanatory power of mathematical models.

6.3 FROM MODELS TO ARCHETYPES

If it has been suggested that nurses' aspirations to a form of nursing knowledge identified with the hard, pure, convergent and restricted sciences should be demolished, a way has been left open to discuss what is possible instead. Black's criticism of natural scientists' imprecise use of models does not leave them, or us, without a lifeline. Instead, he attempts to explain what some social scientists would call 'theorizing', but which he describes as the processes involved when there is 'an implicit or submerged model operating in a writer's thought' (Black, 1962). Disliking the term 'metaphor' because of its inappropriate transfer to objects to which it is not properly applicable, Black substitutes the term 'conceptual archetype'. The following account mirrors some aspects of the grounded theorizing process which takes place when, as a qualitative social scientist studying nursing, I attempt to make conceptual connections and to build 'ideal types' of social reality from my empirical research observations:

> 'By an *archetype* I mean a systematic repertoire of ideas by means of which a given thinker describes, by *analogical extension*, some domain to which those ideas do not immediately and literally apply. Thus, a detailed account of a particular archetype would require a list of key words and expressions, with statements of their interconnections and paradigmatic meanings in the field from which they were originally

drawn. This might then be supplemented by analysis of the ways in which the original meanings become extended in their analogical uses.' (Black, 1962).

I believe that the 'black hole theory of nursing' (which we applied humorously in the first instance to the phenomena we observed in our study of nursing following the introduction of general management into the NHS) bears some relationship to the process of analogical extension that Black describes. It would not help in our analysis to call what is described in the following quotation a 'model', although an *analogy* can be seen between the balance of power of the physical forces which apparently maintain some form of equilibrium in the astronomical black hole, and the social forces which sustain nursing's invisibility in its social equivalent; forces which are, incidentally, imperfectly understood in either part of the analogy. The following quotation describes the *process* of analogical extension in which we engaged during our research:

'Our "mulling over" of the meaning of our observations crystallized one day in that flash of insight which characterizes the research enterprise and which we immediately labelled "The Black Hole Theory of Nursing". In general, it appeared that I had been observing nurses many (but not all) of whom seemed defensively unable to see their work within a broad policy context. Philip Strong, on the other hand, had observed general managers and doctors who displayed the most profound ignorance about pressing nursing issues and practice. It appeared that even where nurses had become nationally known within nursing for taking their work forward in creative and imaginative ways, the local general managers and doctors could remain profoundly ignorant of such innovations. We suddenly realized that despite the impressive statistics (half a million workforce in the United Kingdom) nursing is relatively unimportant to government and to managers in comparison with medicine. It was *medicine* that the Griffiths reforms sought to control: *nursing* was merely caught in the crossfire! The tensions to which this situation gave rise – the nursing group locked into the gravitational force of its internal preoccupations, and the others, on the outside, unable or unwilling to look in and comprehend the nature of nursing's dilemmas – seemed to us to be the social equivalent of an astronomical Black Hole.'

(Robinson, Gray and Elkan, 1991)

6.4 FROM ARCHETYPES TO CONCEPTUAL ANALYSIS

Developing an analogy helps us to make the crucial distinction between 'as if' rather than 'as being' statements, and towards the end of his critique Black refers to what he describes as the existential use of models. If we use language appropriate to the model in thinking about the domain of its application we can work, according to Black's thesis, not *by* analogy but *through* analogy. Hence, considering the forces which help to hold nursing trapped in its invisibility has led me to think a great deal about the distribution of power and control both within and without the profession. Thinking in new ways is always painful, and one's articulation of the issues feels crude and clumsy. Nevertheless, once one has begun to develop an argument around a particular 'frame of reference' it becomes much easier to marshal one's thoughts in coherent ways. Lukes' (1986) radical, three-dimensional view of power has helped me to see that one of the major forces which keeps nurses 'locked in' to the 'black hole' concerns 'the sheer weight of institutions' (Lukes, 1986) which serve to shape their cognitions, perceptions and preferences. As a result:

> '... they accept their role in the existing order of things, either because they can see or imagine no alternative to it, or because they see it as natural and unchangeable, or because they value it as divinely ordained and beneficial. To assume that the absence of grievance equals genuine consensus is simply to rule out the possibility of false or manipulated consensus by definitial fiat.'

> (Lukes, 1986)

Lukes' conceptual analysis of nursing policy issues has continued to be applied both in my own research and in a re-examination of other authors' work. In a recent chapter on Power, politics and policy analysis in nursing (Robinson, 1991), thinking about Lukes' three-dimensional view of power helped in the development of a conceptual categorization of the empirical evidence contained in White's (1985, 1986, 1988) three volumes on *Political Issues in Nursing*. This following provisional categorization involved a great deal of painful conceptual development but, at the same time, yielded an extremely useful framework with which to begin to analyse the powerful tensions which exist within and without nursing:

1. Nursing as a force for challenge and change: the costs and benefits of unity;
2. Contemporary health policy initiatives: the potential risks and benefits for nurses and their clients;
3. The structure of nursing: its constraints and its potential for development;
4. Class, gender and race in nursing;
5. Nurses as oppressors and enablers: power for and against the client.

(Robinson, 1991)

Knowledge is never static and in the chapter cited at (5) above an attempt is made to convey to readers both how isolating and how painful the process of conceptual development can be for the individual concerned, and also how tentative is the resultant framework. Nurses sometimes have an unfortunate tendency to seize on such analyses as though they are written in stone, and not to see that subsequent challenge and reconceptualization is an essential part of knowledge generation. It is important, however, to recognize the ancestry of such ideas and to see how its genealogy can be traced – in the above case, to Lukes' work and beyond. Another simple, but extremely fruitful, framework for conceptual analysis of nursing issues was developed by Stacey (1976). It has helped me to classify nursing according to the conceptual dimensions of health that implicitly underpin different aspects of nursing practice. Stacey argues that health in western society can be conceptualized along each of the three following dimensions:

1. Individual or collective;
2. Functional fitness or welfare (care);
3. Preventive, curative, ameliorative.

It does not take a very great leap of the imagination to see that the nurse who practises along the individual functional fitness, curative dimensions will hold a very different world view of nursing practice and health care intervention from one whose framework involves the collective, welfare and ameliorative dimensions. This analysis may help us to turn conflict between nurses into understanding – a process which is not helped by the pretentious and inappropriate use of the term 'paradigm'. What is required in the analysis is progressive conceptual clarification, so that the various sources of knowledge on which nursing draws may be identified, together with their forms of application in the delivery of nursing care.

6.5 CONCLUSION: KNOWLEDGE GENERATION AS A SOCIAL PROCESS

In the introduction to this paper it was asserted that, although we may apply the findings of natural science in our practice, the activity of nursing is a social process. Therefore its study and understanding will involve the use of social investigation. Furthermore, some nurses, I would contend, have 'painted themselves into a corner' by their inappropriate appropriation of natural science terminology for the academic study of their activities. In a seminal paper, Schutz (1962) helped to clarify many of the dilemmas that flow from what I believe may be described as a category mistake:

> '... authors are prevented from grasping the point of vital concern to social scientists by their basic philosophy of sensationalistic empiricism or logical positivism, which identifies experience with sensory observation and which assumes that the only alternative to controllable and, therefore, objective sensory observation is that of subjective and, therefore, uncontrollable and unverifiable introspection.'
>
> (Schutz, 1962)

Schutz continues:

> '1. The primary goal of the social sciences is to obtain organized knowl-
> edge of social reality. By the term "social reality" I wish to be under-
> stood the sum total of objects and occurrences within the social cultural
> world as experienced by the commonsense thinking of men living their
> daily lives among their fellowmen, connected with them in manifold
> relations of interaction. It is the world of cultural objects and social
> institutions into which we are all born, within which we have to find
> our bearings, and with which we have to come to terms. From the
> outset, we, the actors on the social scene, experience the world we live
> in as a world both of nature and of culture, not as a private but as an
> intersubjective one, that is, as a world common to all of us, either
> actually given or potentially accessible to everyone; and this involves
> intercommunication and language.
>   2. All forms of naturalism and logical empiricism simply take for
> granted this social reality, which is the proper object of the social
> sciences. Intersubjectivity, interaction, intercommunication and lan-
> guage are simply presupposed as the unclarified foundation of these
> theorists. They assume, as it were, that the social scientist has already
> solved his fundamental problem, before scientific enquiry starts.'

In conclusion, it has been argued that the use of the term paradigm in
relation to nursing knowledge is an inappropriate distraction. Developed
originally in order to contribute to a specific understanding of major
theoretical shifts in physics, transfer of the term 'paradigm' to the unre-
stricted, divergent and applied forms of knowledge needed in nursing is
not helpful. Nevertheless, *thinking* about paradigms may be a useful
intellectual exercise, for that cognitive process has helped to bring order
to my own long-standing conceptual jumble. Finally, however, it is necessary to return to the modest approach to the elucidation and generation
of knowledge for practice advocated by Olive Stevenson. Ever-increasing
conceptual clarification in order to describe with rigour the social processes of nursing activity may not be sensational, but it may be all that is
available to us in our current stage of knowledge development. If this
process helps us to better understand, explain and negotiate our way
around the nursing and health care world, then it is probably no mean
achievement.

POINTS FOR DISCUSSION

Robinson's paper attempts to straddle the divide between the conceptual
analysis of events and actions and those methods selected by researchers
as a way of unfolding or elucidating knowledge. That she began her
presentation by admitting that she had a problem with the title
and particularly the use of the word paradigm is in itself an important

starting-off point. Her anxiety with such terminology related first to the inappropriate and often inaccurate usage of terms such as paradigm and model, and secondly to the more profound issue of equating such terminology to the natural sciences. Nursing, Robinson argues, is historically, culturally, socially and politically influenced and therefore cannot select concepts from the natural sciences in isolation from other variables. There is also the problem of trying to explain everything in nursing according to one perspective before nurses have a chance to describe it properly.

A related concern was the realization that there exists a profound ignorance of nursing matters in health care and health policy arenas in general. Robinson graphically describes this as the 'black hole' theory of nursing, where 'nursing is locked in the gravitational force of its internal preoccupations and on the outside (others) are unable or unwilling to look in and to comprehend the nature of nursing dilemmas'. None of this is helped by the inappropriate use of words such as paradigm; what is needed is much clearer conceptual clarification of nursing issues.

The following discussion focused on a number of main themes emerging from the paper. The first series of questions related to whether researchers actually realized that they were involved in conceptual clarification when they undertook a (nursing) study, and if so was it an overt or covert awareness? Her response was that for the most part she felt that researchers were engaging in conceptual clarification in a covert way, but that if one were to look back over the past 15 years of nursing research then it is clear that conceptual developments have taken place.

Another participant asked when was it (ever) appropriate to use the language, metaphors and techniques of natural science, given their limitations in relation to answering nursing questions? If it was the only medium understood by other professionals, could one be justified in compromising one's own conceptual framework in order to elicit cooperation, support and understanding from other groups (and get out of the black hole)?

Robinson's response to these questions was that one could use the traditional scientific method so long as one was cautious and rigorous, and realized that very rarely would one be comparing like with like. She gave an example of trying to compare the effectiveness of a medical intervention involving diabetic patients to nursing interventions as the same client group undertaken by specialist nurses. Of course an experimental design could be drawn up, but the major confounding factor was that one would not be comparing similar events so why not go for an ethnographic case study in the first place?

The issue of presenting 'perverted' data or having to compromise on one's own methodology in order to have the idea accepted, was explored in relation to the use of manpower data and mathematical modelling. Unless one makes assumptions about the predictability and stability of social reality, such modelling is highly suspect. So should nurses accept such methodologies or should they reject them? This question raised the whole issue of power and control within the social arena and how nursing moves out of its invisible mantle and becomes a much greater social force. Such changes were felt to rest on the work done by nurses to clarify their concepts and present them in a palatable way to the public. This was seen as the primary task; learning research methodologies was a second-order activity. What was essential was to begin to clarify what matters in nursing patients.

REFERENCES

Becher, T. (1989) *Academic Tribes and Territories: Intellectual Enquiry and the Cultures of Disciplines*, Society for Research into Higher Education, Milton Keynes, Open University Press.

Black, M. (1962) *Models and Metaphors*, Ithaca, University of Cornell Press.

Bulmer, M. (1982) *The Uses of Social Research. Social Investigation in Public Policy-Making*, Contemporary Social Research, No 3. London, George, Allen and Unwin.

Eriksson, K. (1989) Caring paradigms. A study of the origins and the development of caring paradigms among nursing students. *Scandinavian Journal of Caring Sciences* 3 (4) 169–176.

Kuhn, T. (1962, 1970) *The Structure of Scientific Revolutions*, 2nd ed, International Encyclopaedia of United Science, 2:2. Chicago, University of Chicago Press.

Lukes, S. (1986) *Power: A Radical View*, London, Macmillan.

McFarlane. J. (1986). The value of models for care, in *Models for Nursing*, (eds B. Kershaw and J. Salvage) Chichester, John Wiley and Sons.

Regis, E. (1987) *Who got Einstein's Office? Eccentricity and Genius at the Institute for Advanced Study*, London, Simon and Schuster.

Robinson, J. (1982) *An Evaluation of Health Visiting*, London, CETHV/ENB.

Robinson, J. (1987) Working towards the targets. *Senior Nurse* 6 (3) 24–28.

Robinson, J. (1991) Power, politics and policy analysis in nursing, in *Nursing: a Knowledge Base for Practice*, (eds A. Perry and M. Jolley) London, Edward Arnold.

Robinson, J. Gray, A. and Elkan, R. (1991) *Policy Issues in Nursing*, Milton Keynes, Open University Press.

Schutz, A. (1962) Concept and theory formation in the social sciences, in *Sociological Theory and Philosophical Analysis*, (eds D. Emmet and A. MacIntyre, 1972)

Stacey, M. (1976) Concepts of health and illness: a working paper on the concepts and their relevance for research. Paper produced for the Health and Health Policy Panel of the SSRC. University of Warwick (Mimeo).

Stevenson, O. (1974) Knowledge for Social Work. *British Journal of Social Work* 1 (2) 225–237.

Törnebohm, H. (1985) Tutkijan maailmankuva ja strategia suomalaisissa hoitotieteen väitöskirjoissa - tieteenteoreettinen sisällönanalyysi. Oulun sairaanhoitooppilaitos, tutkielma.

White, R. (1985, 1986, 1988) *Political issues in nursing*, Chichester, John Wiley and Sons.

7

Defining health needs and the need for nursing

Alastair M. Gray

7.1 INTRODUCTION

Although 'need' appears twice in the title of this paper, it must be said at the outset that economists feel uncomfortable with the concept (Culyer, 1976; Williams, 1978). This unease arises largely because need implies an absolute, whereas economic analysis tends to deal in relatives, especially the relative balance of supply and demand. To take a famous example, we need water far more than we need diamonds, yet diamonds cost a great deal of money while water is comparatively cheap; the (economist's) conclusion is that the concept of need is of far less help here than the concepts of supply and demand: there is a plentiful supply of water relative to demand, so the price is moderate, but diamonds are scarce in relation to the demand, so the price is high.

Similar arguments might be encountered in health care: the clinician, politician (but only in opposition) or nurse argues that more resources must be committed to health care because needs are going unmet; yet the level of unmet need does not appear to diminish over time, despite very substantial increases in health care resources, and indeed unmet needs expand with every medical advance. Moreover, numerous studies have demonstrated that almost the entire population has some form of medical condition which could be regarded as treatable, and which might therefore feasibly indicate the existence of a need, yet only a tiny fraction of these seek or are receiving any form of treatment. (Banks *et al.*, 1975; Wadsworth *et al.*, 1971) Thus, if the existence of some unmet health care need was to be the chief criterion for deciding whether to allocate additional resources to health care, we would soon find that the entire gross national product was being committed to this sector.

A small empirical illustration of the relevance of the concept of demand and the problems of the concept of need in relation to nursing is given in Figure 7.1, which shows the relationship between the number of nurses per person and the gross domestic product per person in a number of countries in the Organization for Economic Cooperation and Development: the OECD, sometimes referred to as the 'rich man's club'.

It is quite clear that the level of nurse provision and of natural wealth are closely related: richer countries have more nurses, poorer countries have fewer. If the figure was to be extended to the left, in order to include countries with very low GNP per head and correspondingly high levels of mortality and morbidity, we would find that levels of nursing were generally very low indeed. So, on this evidence, there is no obvious connection between health needs and the need for nursing care; rather, as income increases so does the *demand* for nursing.

It must be recognized, however, that the notion of need does usefully raise two important issues in the context of health care. First, it poses the question of who decides whether a need exists. Individuals may be good judges of how they feel, but measuring, quantifying and/or aggregating this information across groups of people requires a social scientist, an epidemiologist/or some other 'expert'. Individuals are even less well

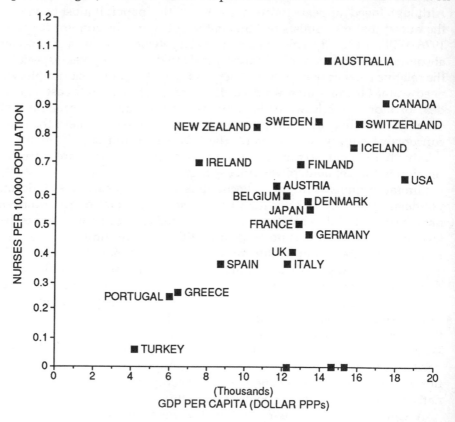

Figure 7.1 Relationship between GDP per capita (PPP) and nurses per 10 000 population, 1987.

placed to judge which kind of health care intervention is most appropriate to their need, or to assess the likely health benefits and costs associated with an intervention. They rely for this kind of information on the provider, notably the doctor but possibly the nurse, therapist or other supplier of health care. This clearly places the provider in a position of great influence, being uniquely qualified to claim the role of determining other people's needs on their behalf; perhaps – at the risk of sounding over-cynical – this is one reason why the concept of need is so attractive to health care providers.

Secondly, and following on from this, the wide currency of the concept of need in health care does implicitly lend recognition to the fact that health care in many ways is not a conventional market in which consumers and producers interact through a mechanism of demand and supply. Economists have identified a number of ways in which the market for health care breaks down or is imperfect (McGuire *et al.*, 1988), the most important being, as noted above, that the consumer has insufficient information (or may be physically/mentally unable) to select appropriate health care, and has to rely on the much better but still incomplete information held by the provider: a parallel might be going to the supermarket and asking the manager to decide what to put in your trolley! It would be difficult to imagine a situation which departs so comprehensively from the notion of consumer sovereignty. In addition, many people view health care as a right which should not be withheld on the grounds of inability to pay, and so we often find that in practice certain types of health care are provided by the state or through compulsory and comprehensive insurance schemes, without regard to the patient's (consumer's) ability to pay.

As a starting position, therefore, an economic perspective might be that the concept of need is useful primarily in drawing attention to the shortcomings of the concepts of demand and supply when applied to health care. This is not to say, however, that demand and supply are irrelevant, or that the health care sector is immune to these forces; rather, it is to suggest that they work themselves out in slower, deeper ways, over longer periods of time, but no less forcibly, like the almost imperceptible grinding of rock and ice in a glacier.

7.2 SOME EVIDENCE ON NURSING SUPPLY AND DEMAND

Some of the changes that have occurred in recent years in the NHS labour force are shown in Table 7.1. After a period of rapid growth during the late 1970s, the number of nurses employed by the NHS in England began to grow at a much slower rate, with a mere 1.1% increase during the 5 years between 1982 and 1987, compared to a 17.8% increase over the entire period 1977–87. As the table shows, other major staff groups have also been affected by this slow-down, but none more so than nursing.

Table 7.1 Growth of health service staff in England, 1977–87

Staff group	Increase (%)		
	1977–82	1982–7	1977–87
Medical and dental	12.4	4.7	17.7
Nursing	16.5	1.1	17.8
Midwifery	2.4	14.0	16.7
Professional and technical	22.6	17.5	44.0
Administrative and clerical	9.9	5.3	15.7
All directly employed staff (Excluding ancillary)	14.5	3.7	18.6

Derived from Health and Personal Social Service Statistics for England, 1989 edition, HMSO, 1989, Table 3.1.

There have also been significant changes over the same period within the nursing labour force, as Table 7.2 indicates: although the proportion of female nurses remained at 90%, the proportion of qualified (registered and enrolled) nurses rose significantly from 49% to 56%, while the proportion of student and pupil nurses fell by almost 7%.

Even larger changes would be apparent if one was to look at a longer period of time. However, I have often discussed these changes with senior nurse managers and planners, and asked if there was any conscious strategy behind them, any long-term plan to increase the proportion of part-timers or alter the qualified–unqualified ratio. The answer has almost always been no: no-one said in 1977 that the proportion of unqualified staff who were part-time should be reduced, or that the rate of growth of nursing during 1982–87 should be the lowest of any major staff group in the NHS. Rather, these changes came about as a series of short-term responses to immediate problems, with no clear end-point in view. Among the problems, we could imagine that a lack of recruits of a particular grade might compel the local nurse manager to recruit another grade; or that a district unable to fully fund a generous pay award to a particular staff group might have to hold back the growth of that staff group or even reduce posts. This brings us back to the influence of supply and demand, and the predictions of economic theory.

Put as simply as possible, economic theory views the production of any good or service as being sustained by a set of inputs: different types of labour and capital. These each have a price, and when the price of any input rises in relation to the others, it would be predicted that production would continue, albeit making less use of the input that has become more expensive, and more use of the input that has become relatively less expensive. The product would not change, but the production process would.

Table 7.2 Changes in composition of the UK nurse labour force

	1977	1982	1987
% Qualified nurses	48.7	51.0	56.0
% Students	24.3	22.4	17.7
% Qualified part-time	34.9	31.5	30.0
% Unqualified part-time	67.3	58.9	57.4

Derived from Health and Personal Social Services Statistics for England, 1989 edition, HMSO, 1989.

This theory assumes that it is usually possible to produce the same good or service with a different combination of inputs, and it also assumes that producers do respond to input prices in order to keep costs of production as low as possible. How realistic are these assumptions when considering nursing in the NHS? In the short term, they probably seem rather unrealistic: it can be difficult to hire or sack employees, the relative prices of different types of labour may not be known, and there are many influences on managers other than a desire to reduce production costs. It could also be argued that the NHS has such influence in the nursing labour market that it can keep wages below the level they might reach in a competitive market, resulting in a perpetual excess demand or 'shortage'.

In the longer term, however, the assumptions underlying the economic theory of production seem more realistic, even in the case of nursing and the NHS. For example, over time staff numbers can be reduced not by sacking but through natural wastage, and managers must eventually give priority to their costs of production, or face difficulties from other managers wanting a share of limited resources or from auditors seeking value for money. Some evidence of long-term changes in factor inputs in the NHS is presented in Figure 7.2. Along the x-axis is plotted the percentage change over the period 1953–1981 in the total amount of working time (that is, taking account of changes in the average working week, the number of full-time and part-time staff, etc.) purchased by the NHS from six broad occupational groups: the increases ranged from only some 22% in the case of domestic and ancillary workers up to around 220% for administrative and clerical workers. The y-axis plots the percentage increase over the same period in pay expressed as an hourly wage rate: this also varied very substantially, from around 900% among administrative and clerical workers to over 1500% among domestic and ancillary workers. Taking the two variables together, it appears that over time they are inversely related: where pay has grown most rapidly the amount of total work time purchased by the NHS has grown least rapidly, and vice versa (Gray and McGuire, 1989).

Hence there does appear to be some evidence that the NHS labour force is not immune to the forces of supply and demand, and that the mix of factors

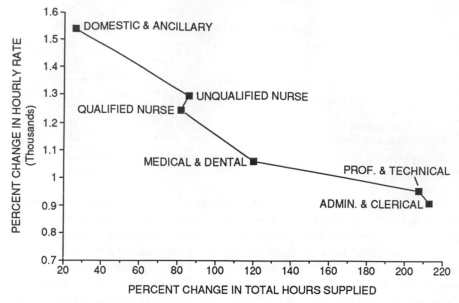

Figure 7.2 Percentage change in wages and work time 1953 – 81; the long term demand for NHS labour.

of production does change broadly in the way economic theory might predict, but incrementally and over lengthy periods. This is in line with previous empirical research, notably from America, that the demand for particular types of health care labour is quite responsive to changes in the relative price of that type of labour: for example, if the pay of licensed practical nurses falls relative to that of registered nurses, hospitals employ proportionately more licensed nurses and fewer registered nurses (Gray, 1987).

7.3 CURRENT NURSING POLICY ON SUPPLY AND DEMAND

When we consider the current debate on nursing supply and demand, it is noticeable that the assumptions about how changes will come about in the future are in striking contrast to the picture sketched above about how changes have come about in the past. Nurses tend to visualize a future in which supply and demand will be brought into balance by means of 'consciously directed policy' (the phrase comes from Richard Titmuss), whereas, as argued above, previous changes occurred in a largely un-planned and unpredictable way. The point can be illustrated by consider-ing the current outlook for nursing supply and demand. The main issues at present are, of course, Project 2000 and the predicted demographic 'black hole'. Demographic changes are producing a sharp decline in the number of school-leavers, who are traditionally a crucial source of nursing recruitment: between 1983 and 1993 the number of school-leavers in England is projected to decline by almost one-third. Meanwhile, it is estimated that the adoption of the education and training strategy set out in Project 2000 may by 1995 have created an annual excess of demand for nurses over potential supply in the region of 16 000.

This problem is depicted in Table 7.3, which shows a predicted annual demand of 32 000 per annum, and a predicted annual supply of 16 000. Table 7.3 also shows some of the actions currently being considered by the UKCC to simultaneously reduce demand and increase supply in order to bring about some kind of balance, which might occur around the figure of 22 000 annual recruits.

This approach of attempting to alter directly the levels of supply and demand for nursing is ambitious, especially in light of the track-record of manpower planning, which requires so many assumptions that many commentators have questioned its usefulness. It may be that some of the actions shown in the table will have their desired effect, but this cannot be relied upon, and meanwhile the forces arising from such things as the changing relative price of nursing compared to other NHS staff keep grinding down all attempts to divert or reverse them. For example, substantially improving the pay and conditions of qualified nursing staff may result in a significant increase in the supply of recruits, but it is also likely to result in a reduction in the demand for qualified nurses relative to other groups.

7.4 CONCLUSION

Planning the nursing labour force on the basis of needs assumes a greater degree of control over change than has usually been observed in the past. Perhaps the solution is to adopt policies which attempt, not to displace the forces of supply and demand, but rather to allow them to work more freely. This approach, which has been described as manpower *policy* rather than manpower *planning*, and has been advocated not only in health care but in other areas such as legal services and other professional industries (Stager and Meltz, 1978; Kirsch, 1982), would involve such things as reducing the many institutional obstacles which make it difficult for managers to respond to relative price changes by altering their mix of factor inputs. However, this is a whole new topic which raises many fresh issues, not least that of whose interests should be uppermost in formulating such policies.

Meanwhile, and to conclude on a suitably modest note, it can be accepted that for all the claims that economists make on their behalf, the concepts of demand and supply are not capable of providing an answer to every problem, and perhaps this is especially so in nursing, which operates in areas lacking many of the characteristics of a free market. It has been well said – and by an economist – that demand and supply are just the way in which one particular group of blind people encounter the elephant. This paper has tried to indicate that while the concept of need may usefully point up some of the deficiencies of supply and demand analysis, it does not overcome them.

Table 7.3 UKCC strategy to achieve equilibrium in nursing

Project 2000 Target recruits per annum	32 000
Demand reducing actions	
20% service contribution from students	-2500
2% reduction in training wastage	-900
1% reduction in qualified staff wastage	-6000
2.5% increase in returns to nursing	-1000
Balance	22000
Supply-increasing actions	
Additional mature students	+1000
Additional males	+500
More entrants via wider entry gate	+4500
Traditional supply constrained by demography	16 000

Source: United Kingdom Central Council (1987), Project 2000: Report on the costs, benefits and manpower implications of Project 2000 (Price Waterhouse), London, UKCC.

POINTS FOR DISCUSSION

Following on from Jane Robinson, Alastair Gray's paper began the debate on how health needs are actually identified within a community and how these are then linked with the individual's need for nursing care. Interestingly, what at face value appeared to be a well understood and commonly used term, the concept of need, seemed to raise far more problems than it solved. From an economic point of view the concept is particularly unhelpful, and given the shift of the health service into a market economy where supply and demand are key factors in determining the level of service, it was interesting to explore whether and how health need and the need for nursing could be interpreted.

The relationship between patients' health needs and the supply of nurses did not appear to be a strong one; what seemed to determine the supply of nursing manpower was the relative cost of groups of workers within the whole service. One could not help being reminded of the earlier debate following Robinson's paper of how nurses begin to elucidate more clearly and accurately what the parameters of their service are, as it was becoming quite clear from Gray's presentation that forces other than nursing evaluations of the patients' nursing needs were determining the supply of the nursing service.

The question of where the data come from to determine policy was a main area of debate, and linked with this was a query as to validity and reliability. The relationship between the presentation of such data and policy formulation was at best a tenuous one, with Gray explaining that often the problem was not so much trying to think up different types of policies, but trying to choose which policies were going to be the most effective. Nobody actually knows how to go about reducing wastage rates, or whether increasing pay by 5% or 10% is going to lead to a 1% fall in wastage. Data would, of course, help in formulating better policies, but Gray was of the opinion that it would not alter the underlying trends as he had described them.

Specific questions were raised about how Project 2000 training figures had been arrived at and what impact the EEC single market would have on the trends. From all the discussions it seemed that the crucial element which was missing was a clear description of what nursing actually provides individuals with at critical points in their lives. It was little consolation to know that economic analysis of local government and social services was equally unsatisfactory, with very few clear guidelines as to what works and how. By decentralizing resource allocation to local communities one may begin to more accurately link service requirements with appropriate manpower, but the shadow side of this is the unnecessary replication of services.

In short, there were no easy answers; economic analysis may illustrate trends and patterns in the deployment and use of nurses, but one is still thrown back to the basic, fundamental question of what nurses are actually trying to do for members of society, and would anybody notice if they ceased to exist?

REFERENCES

Banks, M., Beresford, S., Morrell, D., Waller, J. and Watkins, C. (1975) Factors influencing demand for primary medical care in women aged 20–44: a preliminary report. *International Journal of Epidemiology* **4**, 189–95.

Culyer, A. J. (1976) *Need and the National Health Service*, Oxford, Martin Robertson.

Gray, A. (1987) *The Economic of Nursing: a Literature Review*, Nursing Policy Studies Centre, University of Warwick.

Gray, A. and McGuire, A. (1989) Factor input in NHS hospitals. *Applied Economics* **21**, 397–411.

Kirsch, E. (1982) Manpower policy and the legal profession, in *Lawyers and the Consumer Interest: Regulating the Market for Legal Services*, (eds R. G. Evans and A. D. Wolfson), Toronto, Butterworths.

McGuire, A., Henderson, J. and Mooney, G. (1988) *The Economics of Health: An Introductory Text*, Routledge and Kegan Paul, London.

Stager, D. and Meltz, N. (1978) Manpower planning in the professions, in *The Professions and Public Policy*, (eds P. Slayton and M. Trebilcock) , Toronto, University of Toronto Press.

Wadsworth, M., Butterfield, W. and Blaney, R. (1971) *Health and Sickness: The Choice of Treatment*, London, Tavistock.

Williams, A. (1978) Need – an economic exegesis, in *Economic Aspects of Health Services*, (eds A. J. Culyer and K. G. Wright) Oxford, Martin Robertson.

Experimental research in nursing: necessary but not sufficient

Senga Bond

8.1 RESEARCH STYLES

Research traditions, like most other social phenomena, tend to go in fashions. At the present time my impressions are that there is more support for 'softer', more 'in-depth' and 'non-positivist' research in nursing. There are certainly critiques of experimental research in the UK nursing literature (e.g. Greenwood, 1984; Lyne, 1990) as well as in social science generally (Hammersley and Atkinson, 1983) and particularly in feminist research (Acker *et al.* 1983; Roberts, 1981). These critiques stem from a rejection of the positivist traditions of research characterized as reductionist, mechanistic, reactive, controlling and searching for general laws. The methods associated with natural sciences and with a medical model of care (Busfield, 1986) are under threat of rejection because they are regarded as excluding individual meaning from social phenomena as well as human subjective experiences.

In the UK an adherence to the traditions of medical science is being replaced by a professionalizing ideology for nursing, embodying holistic and person-centred approaches taking the perspective of the individual (Salvage, 1990). The same phenomenon can be observed at an international level. Sarvimaki points to the difficulty in making predictions and thinking in terms of general laws in nursing practice. Nursing, she writes, 'consists of interactions between unique individuals, with unique experiences, and it always takes place in unique situations' (Sarvimaki, 1988, p. 465, quoted in Holmes, 1990). Nursing is conceptualized as communicative action which seeks to understand rather than control. Watson conceives of a phenomenological nursing, drawing on the interconnectedness of matter and 'an epistemology that allows not only for empirics, but for advancement of aesthetics, ethical values, intuition and process discovery' (Watson, 1985). Nursing is conceptualized as a human science and derives its methods from the experiential significance of language. It lies at the opposite end of the continuum from the material positivism of medicine.

The current appeal of the 'new nursing' is likely to exert its influence not only on how nursing is conceptualized but also in the adoption of particular approaches to research. It will foster the adoption of methods which, unlike experiments, are non-interventionist, collect data which are naturalistic rather than research-generated, and focus on human processes rather than other kinds of events. The trouble is, that fashions in research often stand in the way of critical and lateral thinking, and party lines fit more with sloganizing than with original work (Silverman, 1989). My own position is what might be termed methodological pluralism and pragmatism. I do not subscribe to the view that research has to be either/or: qualitative or quantitative, dealing with meanings or with externally defined events, analysing naturally occurring or research-generated data. I say that, because I believe that what is important is the credibility of research, the amount of confidence we have in the findings and not the particular methodological and logical tradition that underpins it. Freidson has criticized the subjectivism in research in the sociology of medicine:

'Positivist assumptions have done considerably less damage to the value of sociological research than have the assumptions of other groups. Some have replaced the myth of objectivity with the myth of subjectivity, holding that subjective reality is sufficient for reliability and validity and ignoring and even arguing against, formal methods.'
(Freidson, 1983).

I would make the plea that the same does not happen in nursing; that the methodologically rigorous baby is not thrown out with the positivist bathwater, by those who adhere to other philosophical and methodological rationales. There is a danger that so-called action research is all action, or worse, purportedly atheoretical observation and not research. Adherence to a particular mode of research, whatever that mode may be, is no excuse for an absence of attention to rigour, to critical thought and to theory building. There is strength in diversity, so long as there is rigour. In nursing at the moment we have a strange juxtaposition of striving for theory development, at the middle range especially, yet a virtual absence of theory testing by empirical research and subsequent theory modification.

8.2 THE LIMITS OF POSITIVIST RESEARCH

Rather than become caught up in the posturing of adherents of particular positions, let us accept for the moment that different methods, when rigorously applied, have different strengths and weaknesses and that no method has claims over any other regarding freedom from sources of invalidity. To this end, while I shall endorse the contribution of experimental – and in this I include quasi-experimental research (Campbell and

Stanley, 1966) – there are limits to the extent that I am prepared to subscribe to practices which have come to be associated with 'positivist' research. These include rejecting:

1. That all research should be quantitative, and that only research which is quantitative can be the basis for valid generalizations.
2. That all research should be based on 'official' statistics, surveys or on experimental designs with randomization of subjects.
3. Assuming that social phenomena have the same kind of invariant or standardized properties as physical stimuli, so that their measurement is regarded as a technical rather than a conceptual problem.
4. That data from different sources are cumulative, so that they are regarded as triangulating, with their intersections revealing the true state of affairs.
5. That with increasingly detailed and refined studies it will be possible to specify the causal agents of social action.
6. Having behaviourist rather than an action model of social life, so that manipulation of stimuli or contingencies will result in particular forms of behaviour.

Following on from these then I would say that:

1. Sometimes quantification is useful, whatever the underlying research paradigm. Even in research which is ethnographic or case study in design, the counting of instances of events to test emergent hypotheses is logically no different from counting events in natural experiments (Silverman, 1985). It is not quantification *per se* that is at issue, but what the numbers represent. Without adequate conceptualization giving rise to the operation of counting or otherwise collecting quantitative data, numbers can obscure rather than reveal, and give rise to false security in the quality of findings. Only when there is confidence in what numbers represent do they permit the making of decisions which would otherwise be less well informed.
2. Experiments, as well as the use of official statistics and survey re-search, are not appropriate for all of the research questions appropri-ate to nursing. They exclude the insights and knowledge available from case study, ethnographic and phenomenological research. How-ever, they have their uses as I shall subsequently show.
3. The quality of measurements, their psychometric and other proper-ties, are matters of technical specification but measurement is not merely a matter of making facts more precise. Underlying measure-ment are conceptual and analytical issues which inform.what we regard as facts to be measured. This is no different from qualitative research in which decisions also have to be made on theoretical grounds about what to observe and what to count as facts. Some facts happen to be assessed by measurement instruments, and so quanti-fied, and some do not. At the root is what we choose to define as facts

and the adequacy of how they were obtained, not that they were determined by observation and filtered through the eyes and ears of a researcher rather than by some measurement instrument.

4. All data are context-specific and the more socially sensitive the data, the more they will be influenced by context. Triangulation in its positivist sense seeks to identify the intersections of 'lines' of data, to seek corroborative evidence rather than focus on 'situated actions'. In this, again, there are major similarities between those who use quantitative and qualitative methods. Experimentalists seek to identify sources of difference or control them, at least in a gross sense.

5. Experimental research can be conducted with interventions as the causal phenomena at different levels of fineness. This is particularly the case in heath service research, and also in nursing studies. It does not mean learning more and more about less and less, any more so than qualitative research which may seek to study smaller and smaller social units. While using biochemical indicators of nursing actions (Boore, 1978) may be seen as reductionism, nursing cannot progress without biological knowledge. It is for nursing to define the level of information it needs to operate successfully.

6. Positivist research is tinged with the mantle of elitism, doing research *on* rather than *with* or *about*, social engineering, mechanistically pulling strings so that individuals will behave in certain ways. While experiments, by their nature, need to have controls, I would argue that the information produced by experiments places individuals in a better position to be able to make decisions, so long as the facts produced are valid. However, attention needs to be paid to the process of informing participants in experiments – so-called informed consent, – as well as the conditions subjects are asked to accept.

Others have also recently considered how experiments with human subjects, if conducted appropriately, are useful. They include nursing, (Wilson-Barnett, 1991), a feminist critique (Oakley, 1990) and sociology (Silverman, 1989).

8.3 SCIENCE, RESEARCH AND EXPERIMENT

Because experimental research evolved in the physical sciences it has come to be labelled *the* scientific method, and because of the ways that other methods and disciplines are regarded, some do not consider them as sciences. Thus we have an Economic and Social Research Council by decree of the then Secretary of State for Education, where formerly we had a Social *Science* Research Council. Nursing is still seeking to establish itself as a discipline, although its relatively recent adoption into some universities now gives it that status. However, like many other disciplines it straddles science, humanity and art. Therefore the characteristics of nursing as a discipline and the methods appropriate to its study are equally diverse, and there is no one empirical method which has an overriding claim to being scientific or more scientific than others. Science itself is a social construct.

Our knowledge of experimental research can be traced to its roots in laboratory science as well as the major advances made in the conduct of agricultural trials by Fisher in the 1930s. Let me take a medical example which antedates this to introduce experimentation. The case is that of Semmelweiss dating from 1844 (see Trusted, 1979). The observation was that women delivered of babies in the First Maternity Division of his hospital had a death rate in 1846 of 11.4% compared with 2 – 3% in the nearby Second Division. Semmelweiss had discovered what he took to be an anomaly, not a chance event or random fluctuation, but a critical observation. It was his knowledge of disease that permitted him to make the observation. What was it about the cases that produced the high death rate in the First Division? He set about suggesting some explanatory hypotheses and used the Second Division cases as 'controls', since he was in a position to manipulate conditions. First of all he could reject some possible explanations. It was not due to an epidemic because it had not spread, nor to overcrowding since there was more overcrowding in the Second Division, for the obvious reason that people preferred to go there. They had the same food, and while the First Division patients were treated by medical students and those in the Second Division were treated by midwife nuns, they had the same training, so he decided that this was not the causal agent. So none of these needed to be changed.

He suggested other hypotheses which he systematically tested: changing the position in which the women were delivered in the First Division to match that in the Second. Was it the priest who came through the First Division to attend the women and the attendant ringing bell that alarmed the patients and so frightened them into getting the fever? He changed the priest's manner of arrival and no difference was obtained. And so on until 1847, when a new hypothesis presented itself from chance observation of a colleague who punctured himself with a dirty scalpel while doing an autopsy, and displayed the same signs as puerperal fever. This was before the role of microorganisms was understood and Semmelweiss came up with the hypothesis that because the medical students came straight from the dissecting room to attend the women in labour, they brought with them 'cadaveric matter' which caused the infection. Thus he asked them to wash their hands in chloride of lime, which he knew would destroy the dead tissue, before attending women in the First Division. The result was a drop in death rate to 1.27%, compared with 1.33% in the Second Division.

The combination of experience and insight revealed a significant difference between the two divisions at the outset, and patient methodical and repeated experiments linked infection with the causal agent. So, while critical observations of anomalies may be insightful, active experimentation was necessary to extend understanding of the critical phenomenon. Unfortunately, the experiment went on to further confirmation when 12 women were purposely examined with dirty hands and all died of puerperal fever. There are other recent examples of experimental and quasi-experimental research where there is violation of ethical principles (e.g. the cervical cancer study in New Zealand (Paul, 1988). The consequences of not randomly allocating patients was brought home in the recent study of the British Self Help Centre. After publishing results indicating a poorer outcome for patients using the centre compared with traditional medical treatments (Bagenall *et al.*, 1990), it was subsequently discovered that the self-selected groups were not equivalent in their cancer staging and that the group were, in fact, more advanced (Chilvers *et al.*, 1990). Their like caused experiments of all types to fall into disrepute. It is a matter of balance. Once again the baby may be thrown out with the bathwater if, because of notorious cases, all experimental research is disregarded or avoided. It is a question of whether, with appropriately rigorous ethical constraints and methods, the net gains to be made from experimental research are sufficient to justify them.

The conclusion to the Semmelweiss tale is that his medical colleagues refused to believe his evidence and eventually the 'cognitive dissonance' he experienced drove him insane.

8.4 WHAT DO WE GAIN FROM EXPERIMENTS?

How and why do people become convinced by experiments? Because experimental data may be contradictory, so some selection of 'reliable' or 'credible' results is necessary. This directs attention to the context in which experiments are performed and used to make judgements about them. Atkinson (1990) has recently examined the evidential basis of ethnographic research. The same requires to be done for experimental research generally and in nursing. What can nursing, in the sense of advancing its knowledge base, gain from experiments?

1. Nursing can substantially gain if experiments are set up in such a way that they add to theory. The inescapable predicament is that we cannot prove a theory or other causal proposition. Empirical research is about trying to expand the number, range and precision of confirmed predictions, and so reduce the number of rival explanations. For nursing theory to develop, we need to generate testable and falsifiable hypotheses and eliminate rival hypotheses. Alternative theory and discordant facts together are necessary to prompt change.
2. Experiments should add to a cumulative body of knowledge relevant to nursing, and in so doing permit theory-based generalizations from the particulars of the experiment to other well defined populations or settings.

3.   As an applied discipline we should expect reports of experimental research to indicate something of the implications of the findings for policy and practice.

While these are what I might be seeking from experiments, what confidence can we have in them?

Because nursing does not operate in closed systems there are numerous extraneous forces likely to 'interfere' with the conduct of experiments. Because we can never know what is true, we have always to use the term 'approximate'. The connection between antecedents and consequents are therefore probabilistic and fallible rather than inevitable. This has to be 'good enough' since practically and philosophically we cannot achieve a complete causal understanding of particular events. In deciding whether the findings of experimental research are sufficiently good to be believed, concern is with assessing how reasonable it is to assume that particular manipulable causes usually produce a given result. What confidence can we have in attributing particular outcomes to particular antecedents and over what time interval? Additionally, as a different issue, how long does the effect persist?

As I mentioned earlier, reductionism is one of the negative feature of positivism. How necessary is it to specify all of the conditions that make up the causal antecedent? Do we need to understand that an antecedent produces a particular effect, or understand why? Simple causal explanations are more about knowing *that* than knowing *why* in the sense of reductionist and essentialist causal explanations. Knowledge of what is likely to happen if something is systematically varied, be it the kind of support women have in pregnancy (Oakley, 1990) or the kind of staff (Paykel and Griffith, 1983), is of great practical significance. Without causal knowledge can we bring about desired states? Or eliminate undesirable ones? Knowledge of causal manipulanda, however tentative, partial and probabalistic, has the possibility for improving social life in general and the quality of nursing in particular, even if we only know that something has an effect rather than why it does, and which only sometimes brings about intended effects.

To follow the experimentalist route would demand increased research efforts. The contingency variables on which causal impacts co-depend would improve in specification, and our knowledge of causal relationships would improve in reliability. It is this form of reductionism with which I have difficulties: experiments are necessary but are not sufficient. For our purposes we often have to get inside the 'black box' and experiments are not inevitably the way to do so.

8.4.1 Doing experiments

When we experiment we isolate as far as possible a theoreticized mechanism to see whether it does what the theory predicts it should do. Experiments are not constructed to see what might happen or to obtain more reliable statistics or more probable empirical regularities. We experiment because we believe that causes operate and have measurable effects, even in the absence of experimental closure.

8.4.2 Possibilities for experimental research

Apart from the ethical considerations, what can we learn from Semmelweiss' pioneering work? Is it possible to adhere to the basic requirements of experimental research in nursing contexts? The list of requirements and some of the problems in their application are listed in Table 8.1.

Having identified what experiments should contribute to nursing knowledge, and noted above some of the constraints in setting up experiments to do so, I will now present the results of a little piece of analysis

Table 8.1 Experimental conditions in nursing research (After Cook and Campbell, 1979, p11)

1. The necessity of a hypothesis as to the outcome of the experiment. The necessity may not be fulfilled, but it has guided the conduct of the experiment.	1. There is nursing theory at the stage of offering hypotheses for testing. How many researchers have the necessary insights based on close observation and informed hunches to create hypotheses worth testing?
2. The introduction of some kind of change.	2. Nursing has limited freedom or will to introduce the changes that theory or insight indicate are warranted to test hypotheses.
3. An isolation of the phenomena under investigation from external sources of influence.	3. In nursing settings we cannot create the controlled environments of laboratories and there are numerous known as well as unknown sources of influence.
4. Dependent variables that are inert and would not be expected to change over time for reasons other than the cause under investigation.	4. The dependent variables that nurses are interested in are sensitive to numerous other effects.
5. There exist explicit and precise theories which specify the exact size of an expected effect and so influence the number of observations necessary.	5. Our theorizing remains so inexact that we have difficulty in identifying relevant causes, never mind the size of their effects.
6. Measurement instruments are available whose calibration and usage is so finely tuned relative to the size of the predicted effect that repeated tests can be made of how closely the observed data fit the expected pattern.	6. Our tools, where they exist, are often crude and insensitive in relation to the size of anticipated effects. There are few examples of repeated tests or replication.

Experimental research in nursing

Table 8.2 Contents of two journals

Journal	Number of papers	Percentage of whole
Journal of Advanced Nursing 1990		
Survey research	61	34
Literature\debate	52	29
Ethnographic\case studies	26	14
Experimental\quasi-experimental	23	13
Methodological	18	10
	180	100
International Journal of Nursing Studies 1990		
Survey research	4	14
Literature\debate	16	55
Ethnographic\case studies	1	3
Experimental\quasi-experimental	6	21
Methodological	2	7
	29	100
Journals Combined		
Experimental\quasi-experimental	29	14

in the survey tradition. I decided in the time I had available to examine the contents of two nursing journals over the last available complete year. These were the 12 monthly issues of the *Journal of Advanced Nursing* (JAN) and the four quarterly issues of the *International Journal of Nursing Studies* (IJNS). I did a crude breakdown of the kind of material published there and the methods that were used in empirical studies. Table 8.2 shows what I found.

Now, any classification is arbitrary. For example, I included in the non-empirical section a paper by Mulhall (JAN 1990) which includes an 'overview' of descriptive, survey and laboratory experimental research in biological and other sciences which are relevant to nursing. Just to show how disappointing titles can be when they are so promising in their first effect, one of the two papers with experiment in the title (Platt, JAN 1990) turned out to use experiment in the everyday sense of something new. It comprised a description of some of the changes introduced and how they were brought about, as well as how participants felt about them: in itself a useful thing to do, but it happened not to fit my purposes. The methodological papers included both quantitative and qualitative methods, and I chose to keep them separate since, for example, the scales being developed may eventually contribute to either experimental or survey work.

Further caution is warranted: one of the claims to validity of survey research is the representativeness of the sample. Because of my sampling strategy, based on pragmatic grounds, I found that a whole issue of IJNS

(November) was devoted to describing research resource developments in a number of different countries. Given these influences, we see that in JAN almost 3 in 10 articles are not empirical, and that 13% are experimental or quasi-experimental. In IJNS over half are not empirical and a higher proportion – one-fifth – are experimental or quasi-experimental. This gave me 29 papers in my sample, 10 of UK origin.

I outlined above the criteria by which we might judge the confidence in the findings, and went on to apply them to these papers; here I offer some general comments based on my analysis.

Table 8.3 Examples of types of research questions asked

	Author	Journal
Hypotheses:		
With direction of effect indicated		
Group 1 would demonstrate significantly higher post-hospital subjective and objective functional capabilities than group 111	Wong et al.	IJNS
Patients who participate in a structured education programme on warfarin sodium prior to discharge demonstrate a higher level of knowledge of factors necessary to safe, effective therapy than patients who participate in an unstructured programme.	Wyness	JAN
With direction of effect not indicated		
There is a significant difference in the frequency of stresses experienced by AIDS patients in special care units compared to AIDS patients in integrated units.	Van Servellen	IJNS
No hypotheses:		
— To describe the effect if the triage system on waiting times for A & E attenders.	Mallet & Woolwich	JAN
This might be reflected in their reported stress levels and job satisfaction.	Long *et al.*	JAN

The necessity of a hypothesis

Experiments should have a formal hypothesis. Most of the studies did not set out a formal hypothesis to be accepted or rejected, although as shown in Table 8.3 a few did so. In some studies a hypothesis with specification of the direction of findings, rather than just a difference, could have been set up, and in others there was an obvious expectation of what the results should have been but no hypothesis was stated. Even Gortner's well designed study hedges its bets by stating 'Our purpose was to determine whether the combined ... *might* enhance ...' (JAN, 1990, p. 1133, italics added) rather than predicting that it *would* enhance.

The majority of papers can better be described, and describe themselves, as evaluations. Evaluations of new products, or of methods of organizing the nursing service or providing care or education. All were sufficiently structured to specify dependent variables, but the research questions asked were tentative rather than formal hypotheses. A study by Freda *et al.* (JAN, 1990), for instance, examines the effects of an intervention to bring about changes in lifestyle among women at risk of preterm birth, and Roe (JAN, 1990) tests the effects of education on patients' knowledge and acceptance of catheters. In both, the direction of expected effects on dependent variables could have been made explicit. While agreeing the need for vigilance to identify unintended consequences for inclusion in subsequent studies, one has to ask why, in setting up interventions in a quasi-experimental design, there is so much caution in prediction.

Theoretical underpinning for the studies and theory-based generalizations

Perhaps I have been narrow here in how I would specify theory, in seeking some explanation of concepts and relationships between them. In some studies theory did not figure at all: they were a straightforward test of equipment. However, even in Auerbach's (IJNS, 1990) comparison of sequential versus simultaneous breast pumping, a theoretical concept – women's preferences – was associated with milk volume. Examples of studies that have drawn on theory are shown in Table 8.4.

Table 8.4 Examples of theory used in studies

Theory		Author	Journal
Orem	– self care	Kirkpatrick	JAN
Moos	– social ecology	James	JAN
Komisoruk & Larson	– pain inhibition	Whipple	IJNS
Lazones & Folkman	– stress & coping	Van Servellen	IJNS
		Lepczck	JAN
Bandura	– self efficacy	Gortner	IJNS
Spielberger	– anxiety	Brown	JAN

Some studies were designed to use analytical concepts but not to critically test particular nursing theories. In this I have included a paper by Fawcett (JAN, 1990) in which 'The Roy Adaptation Model was used to guide the design ...'. The work is as yet in progress, but it seeks confirmation of the beneficial effects of interventions to further support the model. Should such support not be forthcoming, the model will require to be reformulated, or as Fawcett says, 'utility ... must be questioned'. Had a Popperian (Popper, 1962) logic been followed the experiment would have sought refutation.

Kirkpatrick (JAN) draws on Orem's (1985) theory, while others draw on theoretical concepts, which have relevance in nursing, directly from other disciplines. Gortner and Jenkins, (JAN, 1990) uses Bandura's (1989) concept of self-efficacy, while for Wade (JAN, 1990), Thompson *et al.* (JAN, 1990) and Roe (JAN, 1990) adjustment to illness has informed the studies. However, concepts were not actually put to the test in an experimental context. They were very much there in the form of background literature legitimating the particular intervention being tested, and used to specify dependent variables.

A more rigorous approach to theory testing, albeit at the exploratory experimental phase, by Whipple *et al.* (IJNS, 1990) begins to examine the mechanisms of the endogenous analgesia-producing system, using labour pain as the substantive focus. The paper comes up with no clear answers but points to ways of systematically testing influences on pain thresholds to account for observed variability.

None of the reports actually forced a reconsideration of theory. If we adhere to Popper's (1962) notions of advancing theory through testing and falsifying its propositions, then this body of research is disappointing in the extreme, since apart from Fawcett's work, no study actually offers a challenge to nursing theory.

Table 8.5 Examples of theory-based generalizations

Application	Concept	Author
Availability of specialist nurse	Adjustment to illness	Wade
Interventions with significant others in surgery	Anxiety	Raleigh *et al.*
coronary care	Patient satisfaction	Thompson *et al.*
Modification of lifestyle in pre menstrual syndrome	Control	Kirkpatrick *et al.*
Postoperative risk reduction	Self-efficacy	Gotner *et al.*

Adding to the cumulative body of knowledge

Given the above observation, what do the studies add to our knowledge? Essentially, because of the practical nature of nursing and the real-life settings for most of the work described, all of the studies have practical relevance. There was only one example of a situation contrived to examine a particular question. Halfens *et al.* (JAN, 1990) used descriptions of patients in pain to assess the influence of nurses' characteristics on their assessment. Actual educational interventions were set up by Armstrong-Esther and Hewitt (JAN, 1990), to assess effects on attitudes, but with no assumptions that they would influence nurses' behaviour, while Hurtig and Stewin (JAN, 1990) examined the differential effects of different kinds of educational technology on students with different death experiences. In these and all other studies, the interventions, as independent variables, were in field settings. Thus there was practical relevance in all of the work reported.

Practical relevance is extended to theoretical generalizations by invoking the concepts used in the studies. For the most part these were left unstated. Examples of such generalizations are given in Table 8.5.

What confidence can we have in the conclusions?

There are many aspects of experimental studies which influence confidence. Randomization of subjects occurred in some form in 10 of the 29 studies. One study expressly avoided randomization because the standard nursing procedure – syringing wax-impacted ears – was the procedure being examined (Lewis-Cullinan and Janken, JAN, 1990). While randomization generally ensures equivalence between subject groups, in some of the quasi-experimental designs there were no control groups and equivalence was achieved in other ways, e.g. by using subjects as their own controls in time series (Auerbach, IJNS, 1990).

There were clear threats to validity regarding the equivalence of groups in several studies. Most often this was due to relying on post-intervention assessments only, without testing the equivalence of subject groups. There were problems of assignment to groups, so that groups were found not to match on critical dependent variables before the intervention took place.

There were examples of confounding variables not being taken into account, for example the 'experimental' group being treated in one hospital while the 'control' was treated in a different one (Lepczyk, *et al.* JAN, 1990). There were examples of poor specification of the independent variable, either because things did not work out as expected or because there was contamination between conditions. It was not unusual for confounding variables not to have been mentioned. In at least one case, when results were not as they would have been wished, Hamrin and Lindenberg (JAN, 1990) predicted that the quality of the intervention was thrown into doubt rather then rejecting the hypothesis. The authors write: 'The study has not been able to prove from a statistical standpoint ...' and 'the intervention programme was found not to have any measurable effect', in neither case explicitly rejecting a hypothesis, since there was none set up in the first place.

Not everyone would agree with decisions taken about how to specify and measure the concepts being examined. When different ways of measuring the same concept – anxiety – provided different results, this created interpretation difficulties (Brown, JAN, 1990).

Most of the studies were small-scale interventions and, as I have observed elsewhere (Thomas and Bond, 1991), small-scale work is not always up to the complexity of what is being sought of it. Not all studies were small-scale however (e.g. Wade, JAN, 1990; Koch, JAN, 1990), and there were no reports of studies with other than very simple designs.

Some researchers were very aware of the limitations of their studies and said so with refreshing honesty. Koch (JAN, 1990) writes of her work described as a trial and evaluation of a clinical career structure. 'In this instance, the role of the evaluator may be seen as providing technical services at the expense of theoretical, philosophical and practical considerations'. Freda *et al.* (JAN, 1990) say of work that they regard as preliminary, 'Although the sample sizes are small and there is no control group, the preliminary results support the probable efficacy of strategies to modify selected lifestyle factors in the women studied ... a case has been established for further work in the area'. This of course raises ethical problems for the researchers in using a control group with the implied knowledge that they are depriving them of probable interventions to improve the chance of a full-term pregnancy. This is not to detract from the necessity of pilot studies to test methods and protocol implementation, but it points to the need for real uncertainty to underpin the need for experimental studies.

The perfect experiment has yet to be carried out, and while these and other threats to validity were present in many of the studies, there were also examples of rigour within simple designs and their implementation to assess the effectiveness of service interventions, if not to test theory.

8.5 PROGRESS IN EXPLANATION

Often it is sufficient to know that something is effective rather than why it is, but our human curiosity will take us further to want to know why. This often means invoking ideas not introduced at the outset. Wong *et al.* (JAN, 1990) go on to provide explanations of their findings in the methods that nurses used in their post-discharge visits; Halfens *et al.* (JAN, 1990) invoke the medical model to explain why nurses differ in the way they assess pain; Whipple *et al.* (JAN, 1990) postulate why there are differences in pain thresholds; Long *et al.* (JAN, 1990) offer that it is the presence of recovering patients that reduces instances of disturbed behaviour in psychiatric wards; Wade (JAN, 1990) suggests why it is that the difference she obtained between patients attended by a stoma nurse and those who were not disappear after a year. Knowing that there was a relationship between variables was clearly insufficient in many studies, Manicas (1989) writes '... relations of quantified variables are not and cannot be explanatory. Rather they are descriptions to be explained and thus count as evidence of the theories and accounts which explain them'.

Arriving at explanations of observed statistical relations in the studies above involved going beyond the data to use knowledge already possessed or generated as part of the research. In effect, it means getting inside the 'black box' that experiments, on their own, keep closed. This is why I regard experiments as necessary but not sufficient: necessary as a way of avoiding harm and introducing possibilities for better forms of care which others may choose to adopt, but not sufficient when the independent variable is as complex as those we are likely to meet in real-life settings. The studies I have described were sometimes able to identify sufficiently specific features of nursing to use as independent variables. Not all studies can do this nor should they seek to. However, where the independent variables are as complex and ill-defined as, for example, primary nursing and team nursing (Thomas and Bond 1991) or as NHS nursing homes and conventional care, (Bond *et al.*, 1989) then not to go inside the black box leaves many more questions unanswered than a single experiment can answer.

Only one paper I found in my selection combined case studies with a quasi-experimental approach, and that was McLeod-Clark, Haverty and Kendall (JAN, 1990). They set out to use smoking cessation as measured by both self-report and urine cotinine as the dependent variable, but examined the nature of the interventions through detailed case studies of nurses' methods rather than relying on only the formal educational preparation that the nurses received to describe the independent variable. Unfortunately, the paper does not go very far in considering relationships between nurses' strategies, patient variables such as motivation, and outcomes in order to explain the findings. However, I see it as one very positive way of dealing with questions which require answers to both that *and* why.

It would be useful if those publishing were to give greater consideration also to those other practical questions: when, where and how to assist those who may just wish to act on their findings and benefit from the hard work that is necessary for experiments to take place at all.

8.6 CONCLUDING REMARKS

Experimental work may have the charge of social engineering laid against it. However, nurses are in the business of making interventions, whether in offering information to allow patients to decide the best course of action or in taking direct action where patients are unable to do so for themselves.

If on the receiving end, I would like to know that what is on offer or what is done are likely to have a reasonable chance of being effective and a minimal chance of doing actual harm. In one of the studies I was alarmed by the experimental conditions, particularly the withholding of an intervention when previous work has established its value. This involved the separation of mothers and their new infants in hospital (Lindenberg *et al.*, IJNS, 1990).

Such are the meaningful questions that nursing should be asking that we need to use a range of methods. However, to be able to explain phenomena, we cannot rely on experiments alone. Experiments with case study and other explanatory integrations are certainly a step forward, but greater strides are needed to extend the quality of our quantitative efforts, in part to the human consequences of taking part in experiments, but also to better quantitative techniques. More sophistication is required in the use of regression and the more specialized techniques of causal modelling. Then, as well as removing the necessity of manipulation and thus experiments, we really would have to spell out the nature of proposed causal relationships. Nursing theory development to explain and predict events in nursing could only benefit.

POINTS FOR DISCUSSION

In this very comprehensive paper Bond seeks to elucidate those benefits to be gained from using experimental design methodology to answer questions in nursing. Importantly, she begins by describing the principles and assumptions underpinning this approach: empirical research requires the testing of a clearly explicated research question or hypothesis, which is based either implicitly or explicitly in a discrete, theoretical area. The purpose of this sort of research is to identify relationships, or as Bond puts it, that (causal) relationships exist rather than necessarily explain why they exist. She suggested that when research asks why such relationships exist, then other methods linked with the experimental approach are worthwhile.

Bond had remarked that nursing preferences in terms of research methodologies would tend towards qualitative research techniques, and suggested that in areas where practitioners were interested in what she termed 'new nursing concepts', that relatively little quantitative research would be carried out. Interestingly, the range of questions following the presentation was less varied than on other occasions, perhaps because for the majority of the participants there was relatively little experience in the use of experimental research designs or indeed interest in them. This is a worthy observation in itself, as it raises important questions about the accuracy of researchers' judgements regarding study design if they do not at least have some appreciation of the strengths and weaknesses of a range of research methodologies. Might nurses be in danger of committing the same sin as they have accused other professionals of committing, namely adhering blindly to one particular methodology (and in this case qualita tive methods) without acknowledging the complementary and equally important role of quantitive research methods? The real issue, of course, is whether researchers are sufficiently disciplined and rigorous in their own research endeavours to ensure that, whatever method is selected, it is used appropriately.

REFERENCES

Acker, J., Barry, K. and Esseveld, J. (1983) Objectivity and truth: problems in doing feminist research. *Women's Studies International Forum* 6(4), 423–435.

Armstrong-Esther, C. and Hewitt, W. E. (1990) The effect of education on nurses' perception of AIDS. *Journal of Advanced Nursing* 15, 638–651.

Atkinson, P. (1990) *The Ethnographic Imagination*, Routledge, London.

Auerbach, K. G. (1990) Sequential and simultaneous breast pumping: a comparison. *International Journal of Nursing Studies* 27, 257–265.

Bagenall, F. S., Easton, D. F. Harris, E. *et al.* (1990). Survival of patients with breast cancer attending Bristol Cancer Help Centre. *Lancet* 336, 606–610.

Bandura, A. (1989) Self-efficacy: toward a unifying theory of behavioral change. *Psychological Review*, 84, 191–215.

Bond, J., Gregson, B. A. and Atkinson,A. (1989) Measurement of outcomes within a multicentred randomized controlled trial in the evaluation of the experimental NHS nursing homes. *Age and Ageing*, 18, 292–302.

Boore, J. R. P. (1978) *Prescription for Recovery: the Effect of Preoperative Preparation of Surgical Patients on Postoperative Stress, Recovery and Infection.* Royal College of Nursing, London.

Brown, S. M. (1990) Quantitative measurement of anxiety in patients undergoing surgery for renal calculus disease. *Journal of Advanced Nursing* 15, 962–970.

Busfield, J. (1986) *Managing Madness*, Hutchinson, London.

Campbell, D. T. and Stanley, J. C. (1966) *Experimental and Quasi-Experimental Designs for Research*, Rand McNally, Chicago.

Chilvers, C. E. D., Easton, D. F. Bagenall, F. S. *et al.* (1990) Letters to the editor: Bristol Cancer Help Centre. *Lancet* 336, 1186–1188.

Cook, T. D. and Campbell, D. T. (1979) *Quasi-Experimentation: Design and Analysis Issues for Field Settings*, Rand McNally, Chicago.

Fawcett, J. (1990) Preparation for Caesarean childbirth: derivation of a nursing intervention from the Roy Adaptation Model. *Journal of Advanced Nursing* 15, 1418–1425.

Freda, M. C., Andersen, H. F., Damus, K, Poust, D., Brustman, L. and Merkatz, I. R. (1990) Lifestyle modification as an intervention for inner-city women at high risk for preterm birth. *J. Adv. Nurs.* 15, 364–372.

Freidson, E. (1983) Viewpoint: sociology and medicine: a polemic. *Sociology of Health and Illness* 5 (2), 208–219.

Gortner, S. R. and Jenkins, L. S. (1990) Self-efficacy and activity level following cardiac surgery. *Journal of Advanced Nursing* 15, 1132–1138.

Greenwood, J. (1984) Nursing research: a position paper. *Journal of Advanced Nursing* 9, 77–82.

Halfens, R. Evers, G. and Abu-Saad, H. (1990) Determinants of pain assessment by nurses. *International Journal of Nursing Studies*, 27, 43–49.

Hammersley, M. and Atkinson, P. (1983) *Ethnography: Principles in Practice*, Tavistock, London.

Hamrin, E. K. F. and Lindmark, B. (1990) The effect of systematic care planning after acute stroke in general hospital medical wards. *Journal of Advanced Nursing* **15,** 1146–1153.

Holmes, C. A. (1990) Alternatives to natural science foundations for nursing. *International Journal of Nursing Studies* **27,** 187–198.

Hurtig, W. A. and Stewin, L. (1990) The effect of death education and experience on nursing students' attitude towards death. *Journal of Advanced Nursing* **15,** 29–34.

Kirkpatrick, M. K., Brewer, J. A. and Stocks, B. (1990) Efficacy of self-care measures for perimenstrual syndrome (PMS). *Journal of Advanced Nursing* **15,** 281–285.

Koch, T. (1990) A new clinical career structure for nurses: trial and evaluation. The South Australian experience. *Journal of Advanced Nursing* **15,** 869–876.

Lepczyk, M. Raleigh, E. H. and Rowley, C. (1990) Timing of preoperative patient teaching. *Journal of Advanced Nursing* **15,** 300–306.

Lewis-Cullinan, C. and Janken, J. K. (1990) Effect of cerumen removal on the hearing ability of geriatric patients. *Journal of Advanced Nursing* **15,** 594–600.

Lindenberg, C. S., Artola, R. C. and Jimenez, V. (1990) The effect of early post-partum mother–infant contact and breast-feeding promotion on the incidence and continuation of breast-feeding. *International Journal of Nursing Studies* **27,** 179–186.

Long, C. G. Blackwell, C. C. and Midgley, M. (1990) An evaluation of two systems of in-patient care in a general hospital psychiatric unit II: measures of staff and patient performance. *Journal of Advanced Nursing* **15,** 1436–1442.

Lyne, P. (1990) The right questions about nursing care. *Nursing Standards* **5** (6), 36–37.

MacLeod Clark, J., Haverty, S. and Kendall, S. (1990) Helping people to stop smoking: a study of the nurse's role. *Journal of Advanced Nursing* **15,** 357–363.

Manicas, P. T. (1989) Explanation and quantification, in *The Qualitative–Quantitative Distinction in the Social Sciences*, (eds B. Glassner and J. D. Moreno) Kluwer Academic Publishers, Dordrecht, The Netherlands, pp. 179–205.

Mulhall, A. (1990) The contribution of the basic sciences to nursing practice research. *Journal of Advanced Nursing* **15,** 1354–1357.

Oakley, A. (1990) Who's afraid of the randomized controlled trial? in *Women's Health Counts*, (ed. H. Roberts), Routledge, London, pp. 167–194.

Orem, D. (1985) *Nursing: Concepts of Practice*, 3rd edn, McGraw-Hill, New York.

Paul, C. (1988) The New Zealand cervical cancer study: Could it happen again? *British Medical Journal* **297,** 533–539.

Paykel, E. S. and Griffith, J. H. (1983) *Community Psychiatric Nursing for Neurotic Patients: the Springfield Controlled Trial*, Royal College of Nursing, London.

Platt, C. (1990) An experiment in psychiatric community care in north Staffordshire: the experience of working with relatives of mentally ill people. *Journal of Advanced Nursing* **15,** 1315–1318.

Popper, K. (1962) *Conjectures and Refutations*, Harper, New York.

Roberts, H. (ed. (1981) *Doing Feminist Research*, Routledge and Kegan Paul, London.

Roe, B. H. (1990) Study of the effects of education on patients' knowledge and acceptance of their indwelling urethral catheters. *Journal of Advanced Nursing* **15,** 223–231.

Salvage, J. (1990) The theory and practice of the 'new nursing'. *Nursing Times, Occasional Paper*, **86** (4), 42–45.

Sarvimaki, A. (1988) Nursing as a moral, practical, communicative and creative activity. *Journal of Advanced Nursing* **13,** 462–467.

Silverman, D. (1985) *Qualitative Methodology and Sociology*, Gower, Aldershot.

Silverman, D. (1989) Telling convincing stories: a plea for cautious positivism in case-studies, in *The Qualitative–Quantitative Distinction in the Social Science*. (eds B. Glassner and J. D. Moreno), Kluwer Academic Publishers, Dordrecht, The Netherlands, pp. 57–77.

Thomas, L. and Bond, S. (1991) Outcomes of nursing care: the case of primary nursing. *International Journal of Nursing Studies* (in press).

Thompson, D. R., Webster, R. A. and Meddis, R. (1990) In-hospital counselling for first-time myocardial infarction patients and spouses: effects on satisfaction. *Journal of Advanced Nursing* **15**, 1064–1069.

Trusted, J. (1979) *The Logic of Scientific Inference. An Introduction*, Macmillan, London.

Wade, B. E. (1990) Colostomy patients: psychological adjustment at 10 weeks and 1 year after surgery in districts which employed stoma-care nurses and districts which did not. *Journal of Advanced Nursing.* **15**, 1297–1304.

Watson, J. (1985) *Nursing: Human Science and Human Care: a Theory of Nursing*, Appleton Century Crofts, East Norwalk, Conn.

Whipple, B., Josimovich, J. B. and Komisaruk, B. R. (1990) Sensory thresholds during the antepartum, intrapartum and postpartum periods. *Internation Journal of Nursing Studies* **27**, 213–221.

Wilson-Barnett, J. (1991) The experiment: is it worthwhile? *International Journal of Nursing Studies* **28**, 77–87.

Wong, J., Wong, S., Nolde, T. and Yabsley, R. H. (1990) Effects of an experimental program on post-hospital adjustment of early discharged patients. *International Journal of Nursing Studies.* **27, 7–20.**

The effects of nursing care: an ethnographic approach

Kath M. Melia

9.1 INTRODUCTION

Since agreeing to take part in this seminar series I have had an experience which could be described as every ethnographer's dream, one which could have led to a paper entitled 'tales from a Greek hospital bed' – rather apt when you look at the origins of the word ethnography (Gk. *ethnos* = a people, a nation, and *graphe* = a writing). A brief explanation of this experience is in order. I was admitted to Rhodes hospital (after a night in our hotel room in Symi with a drip running and a 2-hour sail on the interisland ferry). All this was necessitated by an unprecedented and impressive stomach bleed. I had three units of blood and came closer to departing this life than I care to think about, and was brought home by air ambulance direct to Edinburgh Royal, where I encountered the NHS on a Saturday night.

I mention this experience because it has given me some insights which have a bearing on this paper. First, I am now convinced (I had long suspected) that we need more ethnographic research on the patient's experience of illness and hospital care. As we know little about this, ethnographies of different conditions would be useful. Secondly, and this I had not thought much about before, the patient experience of care comes as a package, it is not broken down along professional fault lines. By this I mean that it is exceptionally difficult to focus upon the work of any one member of the team in order to evaluate its effects. Thirdly, and this is another confirmation of a long-held suspicion, that caring is an activity which is extremely difficult to appropriate and claim as a professional activity. Caring is a problematic concept. I saw care given by relatives in the Greek hospital, they carried out most of the daily routine non-technical nursing. I also saw nursing practice which was almost entirely of a technical nature, the amount of basic, day-to-day care that the nurses gave we would regard in the British context as minimalist. It should be emphasized that this is a cultural difference and no criticism of Greek nursing. I mention it to highlight the problems associated with defining and evaluating professional care.

If I pursue this 'tales from a Greek hospital bed' line much further I am in danger of supplying the evidence for those who do not believe that ethnography is any more than story-telling. I plan to discuss ethnography in very general terms. My invitation to speak suggested that I might consider the generalizability, reliability and validity issues in relation to ethnography. I will go on to examine what we mean by the 'effects of nursing care' and to consider what ethnography has to offer.

9.2 ETHNOGRAPHY

Ethnography is the method of social research which we have come by through anthropology. Initially it was the cultural anthropologists who studied human groups – usually foreign and exotic. The methods have been adopted by sociologists, who employed them in their own societies in order to understand the behaviour and values of groups within the larger society. There are some circles in which the ownership of the method – ethnography and its closely related research techniques, participant observation and fieldwork, – are debated. I take the view that ethnography is the research approach adopted by both anthropologists and sociologists: its purpose not its disciplinary home is what matters. Ethnography, then, is being used here, as elsewhere, as a shorthand for the kind of research that seeks to understand the phenomenon under study from the perspective(s) of the actors in the situation.

Qualitative methods is the term used by Filstead (1970), Bogdan and Taylor (1975) and Glaser and Strauss (1967) for methods where the idea is to get close to the data and to derive explanatory concepts from those data. Participant observation, in-depth interviews and the study of documentary evidence are the means by which these data are acquired. Essentially, the focus of interest is to gain an understanding of the ways in which people understand, interpret and structure their lives (Burgess, 1984). These methods of investigation have been developed in relation to those theoretical perspectives or orientations concerned with the way in which the social world is constructed by the participants. This has been discussed in terms of how individuals experience and construct reality (Berger and Luckman, 1967).

The theoretical tradition of interactionism (Becker, 1958; Blumer, 1969; Hughes 1970) played a part in the development of qualitative methods, with their emphasis upon an understanding of the participants' actions. In Blumer's words, in order to do research:

'One would have to take the role of the actor and see his world from his standpoint. This methodological approach stands in contrast to the

so-called objective approach so dominant today, namely that of viewing the actor and his action from the perspective of an outsider.'

(Blumer 1969)

Schatzman and Strauss (1973) perhaps hit upon the most useful idea when
they described the field researcher as a 'methodological pragmatist', who
sees 'any method of enquiry as a system of strategies and operations
designed at any time for getting answers to certain questions about events
which interest him'.

It is interesting to note that Gerhardt (1989) points out that, despite the
work of Becker, Hughes, Strauss, Roth, Davis and Bucher, all of which was
undertaken employing Mead's interactionist perspective – a perspective
which Mead's students continued after his death in 1931 – it was only with
Goffman's 'compassionate account of the plight of prison inmates and
patients in mental hospitals which caused the breakthrough of symbolic
interactionism' (Gerhardt, 1989). Maybe nursing is still in need of such a
breakthrough!

I think, although one still hears the argument rehearsed, that the qual-
itative/quantitative debate is now sterile. Maybe when nursing regarded
itself as a newcomer to the research scene and looked to the 'hard'
scientific methods and predictive theories in order to gain its research
spurs, maybe then the debate had its place. The central questions now
(and probably then) are what do we want to know? and how best might
we find it out? So, we have to ask what is the nature of the knowledge that
we are after – is it, for instance, knowledge of the physical world or the
social world? The next step is the epistemological one, to ask how do we
know? to ask, what counts as knowledge? and how best we might appre-
hend it? At an operational level these questions present as, what counts
as data? how do we best answer our question? If we are dealing in the
physical world the answer is theoretically reasonably straightforward,
although it may be technically complex (as those who have attempted
measures of wound healing etc. will testify). If, on the other hand, we are
dealing with the social world, the operational means by which we link our
conceptual notions of the phenomena under study to the empirical data
available, is problematic. The Anglo-Saxon question which usually stops
graduate students in their tracks is, 'would you know it if you saw it?' It
being anxiety, stress, good communication, skilled care, whatever the
research focus is.

So, what does ethnography have to offer in the realms of the 'effects of
nursing care'? It is very much a matter of horses for courses. Far more
problematic, I would suggest, is the notion of examining the effects of
nursing care. Outcome measures are notoriously difficult to nail, let alone
measure. Ethnography would probably offer insights and explanation –
not always the stuff of evaluation research.

I would argue that we tend to underestimate patients as a data source.

Professionals tend to set the benchmarks and patients assume that they are in some way failing if their experience does not work out to match.

Ethnography, then, is appropriate for some of the areas of nursing which are not tractable by other means, i.e. the experiment, survey, etc. Ethnography may well play but one part of a multimethod study. I have used the ethnographic approach, employing the informal interview as the means of data collection, to study the student nurse's view of nursing, the interface between hospital and community nursing staff in the care of elderly patients. I am about to start the data collection phase of a study of the moral aspects of nursing work, focusing upon the staff nurse.

The expectations of ethnography should be understood at the outset. In order to shed some light on these expectations I will now look at the issues of reliability, validity and generalizability. Taking the last first, generalizability is really part of the language of the survey methodologist, findings that are generalizable from the sample to the population. That ethnographic work might be replicated is perhaps not so much the point. The thing that is carried forward (and perhaps tested) from ethnographic work would be the theoretical insights it has yielded. Rather than endlessly replicating to see if the findings hold true here and there, the ideas should be taken up in further work and tested, but testing is not the prime goal. This notion of carrying forward the theoretical insights is in tune with Glaser and Strauss (1967) and their idea of 'plausibly suggesting, not empirically testing hypotheses'.

Reliability concerns whether the same 'answer' would obtained by repeated data gathering by independent researchers? Maybe, maybe not; again the concept as we understand it has its roots in experiment and, following it, the survey. This is not to say that ethnography is without rigour; on the contrary, ethnographers tend more to wear their methodological hearts on their sleeves as they cannot resort to Chi squares and graphs for security. There are ways of checking and verifying data throughout the course of an interview or over a period of participant observation (see Brink (1989) for a discussion of this issue, although I think she goes too far in her desire to 'translate' into quantitative language).

Validity is essentially about asking have we got what we thought we were looking for? and do the indicators chosen represent the concepts? We are also concerned with external validity, that is, how far the results can be generalized beyond the study.

Various authors, notably Denzin (1970), have written about the triangulation of methods in an attempt to achieve validity. I do not think that triangulation really offers much in the way of an answer, but it does offer rigour, which is clearly a good thing. However, different methods rest upon different epistemological bases and so, to regard triangulation as something which has any more to offer than bringing further data and analytical ideas to bear on the issue, is to be misled. At the end of the day, however, as is the case with a good deal of social research, we cannot know without a doubt that our interpretation or what we have discovered is how it is, even supposing that there were only one *is*, for multiple realities are part and parcel of life and therefore of analysis.

Morse (1991) notes the reaction of an ethics committee member to her suggestion of a modification of the experimental method in order to lessen the risk for patients, at the expense of experimental rigour. The member said 'but how will you know? you've got to really know!' Morse goes on to say that 'methods often reflect the discipline in which they were developed; these in turn are closely associated with and reflect the values underlying the discipline'. She notes that medicine is concerned with certainty and so is preoccupied with the experiment. Psychologists want to know 'is it replicable?' Social survey research is concerned with representativeness: 'is it generalizable?' In cultural anthropology, Morse says, the question seems to be 'is it interesting?' As she wryly puts it, the ultimate compliment a cultural anthropologist might receive after presenting research output is 'fancy that'. In nursing, Morse says, the most significant question seems to be 'is it good for the patient?' Becker's (1958) classic paper is as good as any on this vexed matter of validity.

Strong (1979) in the methodological appendix of his work has some useful comments on qualitative methods. He is especially helpful on the middle ground between analytical induction and grounded theory. On a wider front he says;

'... insofar as there is any pleasure in the rigours of analysis and writing most of the joy comes from making one small piece fit with another and tidying up all the loose ends (in this respect ethnography has a good deal in common with housework) – these obsessions are rarely shared by readers, who are more concerned with the point of the whole enterprise.'

How, then, do we assess the point of the whole enterprise in ethnography? First, as I have already said, by having realistic expectations of the research approach. Ethnography will yield insights, substantive and theoretical if it is appropriately used – one would clearly not attempt the census by the ethnographic approach! Secondly, we have to accept that however rigorous our methods we cannot know beyond doubt that we have got it right. To quote Strong (1979) again

'Some authors have been so disturbed by the failure to generate foolproof interpretive methods that they have abandoned all interest in conventional subject matters and concentrated solely on analysing the methods that are used in everyday life to this end; their hope being that here at least some certainty is to be found. The more optimistic of them have an essentially Cartesian strategy. They have deliberately suspended the belief in all the things that sociologists normally claim to know, hoping that if some small area of life can be found about which knowledge can be truly generated, than a proper sociology might eventually be constructed on this firm basis. While this quest for certainty has produced some brilliant studies of lay methodology and the structuring of talk, the larger programme is surely a delusion and is likely, despite its rigour, to go the way of the many previous attempts to find an epistemological bedrock. The best we can hope for in this world, even if we study practical reasoning, is a plausible story.'

Ethnography in nursing will give us the 'plausible story' that will serve to explain those areas we choose to discover more about by this method. If we are looking for causal relationships or predictive theories we will, I fear, be disappointed. Some kinds of theory attempt to explain more than others and some theoretical explanations are useful in that they open up the topic for discussion – they provide the conceptual currency with which to have the debate. If, like the medical member of Morse's ethics committee, we are looking to be certain, we will probably be frustrated by ethnography and indeed by the kinds of issues it aims to study.

We are left with the problem of 'how do we *know*?' Like the story about the fridge, how do we know that when we have shut the door the light goes out? Or the family who, when asked what their dog was called, replied 'We don't know, we call him Rover'. How *do* we know? I will settle for Strong's 'plausible story'.

POINTS FOR DISCUSSION

Melia's contribution to the discussions on research methodologies used in nursing focused on the ethnographic approach. Classified as one of the more familiar qualitative approaches, ethnographers seek to answer such fundamental questions as what it is that we need to know about something and how best might we find it out. Documenting the research subjects in their natural environment and seeking to explain their view of the world are basic aspects of an ethnographic approach.

A question raised at the beginning of the discussion was whether ethnography should not in fact try to look for predictions about relationships between cause and effect. It was suggested, however, that ethnography played an equally important role as a method of mapping experiences and providing some sort of conceptual clarity to events. This descriptive process had to precede any exploration of causal relationships and was itself a very demanding activity. For example, one had to be aware of how one could be guilty of differentially weighting the value or importance of different versions of the same event. Let us say that patients and nurses were interviewed about a certain service: how would one ensure that more credence was not given to the nursing (perceived to be a more informed, professional view) than to the relatively uninformed patient view? To seek for corroborating evidence by way of seeking more views on the same subject was one way of ensuring that the theoretical insights plausibly suggested by ethnographers were more likely to be accurate representations of reality.

Ethnography was seen to provide an important means by which nurses could begin to clarify those concepts in nursing which have been resistant to any sort of consistently agreed working definition.

REFERENCES AND FURTHER READING

Becker, H (1958) Problems of inference and proof in participant observation. *American Sociological Review* **23**, 652–660.

Berger, P. L. and Luckman, T, (1967) *The Social Construction of Reality*, Harmondsworth, Penguin.

Bogdan, R. and Taylor, S. J. (1975) *Introduction to Qualitative Research Methods: a Phenomenological Approach to the Social Sciences*, New York, John Wiley.

Blumer, H. (1969) *Symbolic Interactionism: Perspective and Method*, Englewood Cliffs, NJ, Prentice Hall.

Brink, P (1989) Issues of reliability and validity, in *Qualitative Nursing Research: a Contemporary Dialogue*. (ed. J. Morse), Aspen.

Bucher, R. and Strauss, A. L. (1961) Professions in process, *American Journal of Sociology* **66**, 325–334.

Burgess, R. (1984) *In the Field: an Introduction to Field Research*, London, George Allen and Unwin.

Davis, F. (1960) Uncertainty in medical prognosis, clinical and functional. *American Journal of Sociology* **66**, 41–47.

Denzin, N. K. (1970) *The Research Act – a Theoretical Introduction to Sociological Methods*. Chicago, Aldine.

Filstead, W. J. (1970) *Qualitative Methodology: First-Hand Involvement with the Social World*, Chicago, Markham.

Gerhardt, U. (1989) *Ideas about Illness: an Intellectual and Political History of Medical Sociology*, New York, New York University Press.

Glaser, B. and Strauss, A. L. (1965) *Awareness of Dying*. Chicago, Aldine.

Glaser, B. and Strauss, A. L. (1967) The discovery of grounded theory, Chicago, Aldine.

Goffman, E (1968) *Asylums*. London, Penguin Books.

Hughes, E. C. (1970) *The Sociological Eye*. Chicago, Aldine.

King's Fund Centre (1990) *Cancer of the Colon and Rectum*, 7th King's Fund Forum Consensus Statement. London, King Edward's-Hospital-Fund for London.

Melia, K. M. (1987) *Learning and Working: the Occupational Socialization of Nurses*, London, Tavistock.

Morse, J. (1989) *Qualitative Nursing Research: a Contemporary Dialogue*, Aspen.

Morse, J. (1991) Editorial. *Qualitative Health Research* **1**, 1.

Roth, J. (1963) *Timetables*, New York, Bobbs-Merrill.

Schatzman, L, and Strauss, A. L. (1973) *Field Research – Strategies for a Natural Sociology*, Englewood Cliffs NJ, Prentice Hall.

Strong, P. (1979) *The Ceremonial Order of the Clinic*, London, Routledge & Kegan Paul.

10

Action research: philosophy, methods and personal experiences

Christine Webb

10.1 INTRODUCTION

My experiences of clinical teaching over a period of many years in several different hospitals in England had led me to be increasingly dissatisfied with the quality of care and learning experiences offered to learner nurses. The (infamous) theory practice gap loomed very large, both in organizational and clinical practices. For example, there was a lack or misunderstanding of the use of nursing models and the nursing process; work was mainly organized along task allocation lines even where lip-service was paid to patient allocation; technical nursing was carried out in a traditional rather than research-based way; and virtually no overt teaching took place in the wards.

My reading led me to believe that things did not have to be like this. Committed practising nurses have succeeded in introducing systematic care planning to their wards and organizing nursing on a patient-centred or primary nursing basis (Binney, 1986; Sparrow, 1986). There is some evidence that these changes lead to better care and higher staff morale, and increasingly research is providing us with guidelines about how to carry out direct care more effectively (Horsley *et al.*, 1983). Many ward learning environment studies from Revans (1964) and Menzies (1960) through Pembrey (1980), Orton (1981), Fretwell (1982) and Ogier (1982) to Reid (1985) have demonstrated which types of climate and interpersonal style lead to greater satisfaction on the part of nurse learners with their practical experience. Reid's (1985) study has also suggested that learning is enhanced in more positive learning environments, and has undermined the credibility of rationalizations that 'we can't do it because we are so short-staffed' by showing that staff–patient ratios and patient dependency are not necessarily barriers to progressive practices on wards.

In other words, we can do it if we try. It is possible to nurse *patients* and not merely carry out *tasks*, to write detailed care plans which are useful as learning devices for learners as well as documents which record the care given, and to relate to each other at work in mutually respectful and constructive ways. And patients might even benefit too.

At the same time, I was not so naive as to believe that nurses trained to use more traditional methods would find it easy to change without support. Nor did I see structural features in the mid-1980s as irrelevant - patients are more dependent and stay in hospital for shorter times, and nurse staffing levels are more precarious than they used to be.

Action research therefore seemed the ideal way to try to bring about some of the changes I had in mind, because it builds on people's own motivations to change, gives authority to a change programme, and offers support and resources to those trying to develop new ways of working (Towell and Harries, 1979).

10.2 PHILOSOPHIES OF RESEARCH

Quantitative and qualitative approaches to research have frequently been seen as based on opposite and opposing philosophies of science. Quantitative or positivistic research, on the one hand, aims to test hypotheses, use 'objective' measures, and predict and control phenomena. On the other hand, qualitative or interpretive research is concerned with understanding the meaning which actors themselves give to their social lives in order to enhance mutual understanding and cooperation among groups (Fay, 1975). It is useful to distinguish between the two modes in order to understand the historical development of social research, to uncover the underlying assumptions of the two approaches, and to make judgements about which is most appropriate when planning a research project.

However, the distinction between the methods researchers have used when adhering to one or other approach has been overstated. Participant observation and unstructured interviews have been used in the initial exploratory stages of projects and these early findings have then been used to generate structured measuring tools for quantitatively oriented main research projects. Similarly, large-scale structured questionnaires have been followed up by in-depth interviewing of a subsample of respondents to gain richer data than are obtainable by self-completion questionnaires. Methodological eclecticism does not represent a radical change, but involves using different methods in parallel rather than in series, as previously advocated.

10.2.1 Eclectic approach

More recently, an eclectic approach has gained popularity and researchers have emphasized the need for a triangulated approach to data collection (Bell and Roberts, 1984). Triangulation, or use of a variety of methods, leads to a more full and rounded picture of the subject being studied by approaching it from a number of different angles. The 'angles' may be those of different researchers, different methods, different research populations, or a combination of these. Far from being less rigorous and 'scientific', this methodological eclecticism may add validity to research findings because they are based on more comprehensive evidence. This eclectic approach is not simply based on a pragmatic wish for more varied data, but arises from criticisms of the philosophies underlying both positivist and interpretive approaches (Fay, 1975). Quantitative research had been criticized for the naivete of its claims to objectivity and to an ability to use quantitative measures to study subjective phenomena such as anxiety and pain. This style also has authoritarian and paternalistic elements in aiming to produce laws of behaviour which allow control of social phenomena (Susman Evered, 1978). Qualitative styles make no claims to objectivity and generalizability, but place greater weight on interpersonal relationships and communications rather than structural features of society which constrain almost every aspect of our daily lives (Giddens, 1974). Thus both styles of research give incomplete and inadequate pictures of how people behave and the possibilities for social change.

A third kind of philosophy of social research is being advanced by those who wish to go beyond the limitations of positivist and interpretive research in terms both of their philosophies and their methods. Critical research is based on the philosophy that research should not be an esoteric activity indulged in by researchers in isolation from the people they study. Instead, researchers should involve people being studied in planning, carrying out and acting upon research findings so that research becomes a resource that people can use to change their own lives (Fay, 1975). Researchers and their collaborators would then choose the research methods most suitable to the subject under study and the aims of the research, thus taking advantage of the benefits of the eclectic use of methods discussed earlier.

10.2.2 Action research

Research in the critical style includes 'committed' research such as feminist research, peace studies and action research (McCormack, 1981). Action research is increasingly being seen by nurses as an approach which has much to offer because they can use it to analyse problems, devise programmes of action designed to solve problems or improve standards, carry out and evaluate these plans, and learn more about research in the process.

Action research has been used in nursing in a variety of ways. Towell and Harries (1979) acted as facilitators of change in a psychiatric hospital, giving advice and emotional support. They place particular emphasis on the need for support resources for nurses who are trying to introduce changes in their work practices, and see action research as a means whereby staff can 'take back the authority for clarifying their own roles and working to establish the conditions required for effective task performance by themselves and others' (Towell and Harries, 1979).

Lathlean and Farnish (1984) used action research to evaluate a ward sister development project. The researchers monitored the project and fed back their findings to participants so that they could use them to refine and build on what they did within the project.

Hunt (1987) used action research to encourage nurses to use research findings in their work, and evaluated the outcome of the project. Her work was guided by Lewin's conceptual framework, which sees action research as 'a cyclical process of fact-finding, action and evaluation, following which the process begins again' (Ketterer *et al*, 1980). In Hunt's study, nurse teachers became resources for change by finding and using research reports relevant to clinical practice, focusing on mouth care and preoperative fasting. Change was then promoted by means of formal teaching, the procedure committee, supplies department, and involvement of anaesthetists. The innovation met with limited success, due to resistance to change on the part of ward staff who felt more secure adhering to established routines. Again, the importance of support and effective management systems in implementing and sustaining change emerges from the study.

Questions of reliability and validity in action research have been considered by Greenwood (1984) and others. External validity or reliability are not considerations for the researcher carrying out a qualitative case study, according to Elliot and Ebbutt (1983). The responsibility for showing external validity lies with those who wish to use the study findings, and the researcher seeks to produce a 'naturalistic generalization' of what happened in the process of carrying out the project. With a case study approach, which is what action research entails, the emphasis is on collecting multiple representations and the presentation of evidence in forms which are open to multiple interpretation. Control or comparison groups are not part of such an approach, but comparisons are made within the case study by analysing how actors' behaviour, attitudes and knowledge change. Willmott (1975) considers that ideally a balance should be sought between as precise a form of measurement as possible, and a more qualitative exploration and description. Greenwood (1984) believes that the face validity in action research guarantees that findings fit reality, and that reliability can be checked by ensuring agreement between the interpretations of researcher and participants. Lack of generalizability is not a problem because a unique, individual situation is being studied, but some findings may be generalizable to other similar settings.

10.3 PLANS FOR THE PROJECT

Having decided upon action research as the most appropriate approach for the project, I then developed a plan based on the following aims:

1. To use an action research approach to develop nursing and management skills on a hospital ward in order to improve both the quality of patient care and student nurse learning (stage 1:2 years).
2. To use this 'development ward' as a base for training registered nurses in nursing and management skills. These trained nurses would then go to work on their own wards and be in a position to transfer their learning and develop their own wards (stage 2:2 years)

This paper is concerned with the initial phase of stage 1 of the project, which entailed a period of approximately 3 months, during which I worked as a participant observer on the study ward for one shift each week. The aim of this period was both to collect some baseline data which could be used for later comparisons, and for me to become familiar with the ward, its staff and their ways of working.

The action research approach I planned to use was different from earlier projects in which researchers had acted as facilitators or change agents. I planned to work alongside trained nurses on their own ward and use my nursing and teaching experience to help them to evaluate their practice, plan and implement change, and evaluate its effects. Rather than employ special ward sisters and preceptors, as in the Lathlean and Farnish (1984) study, trained staff would take action on their own ward. If successful, this would show that special nurses or researchers were not necessary to introduce innovation, but that 'ordinary' nurses could achieve change when provided with advice and support. The project therefore had implications beyond the individual project ward, and would contribute to the development of action research methodology in nursing.

Following this initial period of observation, the action phase of stage I would then begin, and would necessitate the commitment of the study hospital to providing a 'bank' nurse to give trained staff cover for the ward for 3 hours per week. This would enable me and the usual trained staff to withdraw from the ward for discussions, teaching and planning. I would continue to spend 1 day per week working on the ward to support staff in making the changes we agreed on in our weekly meetings. I envisaged that meetings would have to take place weekly for at least 3 months before any 'action' was taken. This was because it would be important for staff themselves to decide what they wanted to do and how to do it, and then I would provide some facilitative teaching and help them to draw up concrete plans to introduce changes. Only one change should be introduced at a time, and evaluated and modified as necessary. Only when this was established practice should another change be tried. Thus the whole project might take 2 years or longer.

After successful approaches to the district general manager and nurse managers at a district general hospital, a lunchtime meeting was arranged for me to talk to ward sisters about the planned project and invite volunteers to participate. Several sisters explained why their wards would not be suitable, and I agreed with some of their reasons. I knew that I must work on a ward where my clinical credibility would be strong, and therefore a highly specialized setting such as neurosurgery was ruled out.

A sister of a general medical ward volunteered, and the project began on her ward. Action researchers emphasize the importance of volunteering rather than management selection for a project of this kind, because a motivation to change is essential and because the project is inevitably stressful for participants (Lathlean, personal communication).

10.4 PARTICIPANT COMPREHENSION

A key difference between this and earlier studies of the use of action research to facilitate change on hospital wards is the fact that I participated as a nurse and action researcher in the everyday work of the study ward. This method, variously called participant observation, ethnographic research or simply fieldwork, allowed me to appreciate what it was like to be a nurse on the ward, what were the strengths and weaknesses of its present ways of working, and how trained and learner nurses felt about working there.

Participant comprehension is the term used by Collins (1984) in preference to participant observation. He links observation with the positivist, 'objective' form of data collection, which distorts interaction in the field by the very devices it uses supposedly to overcome the researcher effect. By 'hanging around', taking notes and asking questions, the complete observer introduces an artificiality into the situation, both by her own presence and behaviour and by transmitting this sense of differentness to those being observed.

Participant comprehension, by contrast, deals with these problems by abolishing them. The researcher does not have to agonize over how to 'take a role' or disguise in the field, the most efficient but unobtrusive way to take notes, or on how to act so as to minimize distortion. Instead she enters as herself – a researcher whose purpose is known to 'insiders' and who can therefore be openly 'naive' and engage them in discussions about what they are doing and why. The complete observer's ethical as well as methodological dilemmas are solved because the need to dissimulate and deceive is removed. This is not to say, however, that other methodological and ethical issues do not arise, as I shall discuss.

While participating in ward activities I kept field notes of various kinds, as suggested by Glaser (1978). Observation notes were descriptive recordings of events which occurred and conversations which took place. Methodological notes recorded both occurrences which seemed to have methodological implications – for example how staff reacted to my presence – and comments on the use of the methods I had adopted. Theoretical notes were built up as the study period advanced, and I began to detect 'themes' emerging from the data. As patterns emerged, I became sensitized to look for further examples and to build up evidence either to support or contradict my interpretation. Glaser (1978) calls these theoretical ideas 'sensitizing concepts', and my data collection methods were an approximation of the process he describes as 'the discovery of grounded theory'. After formulating categories, the researcher develops these by carrying on looking for evidence until nothing new emerges and a state of saturation arises. The aim is to produce 'a model of social reality … which adequately comprehends the life-worlds of the people being studied, while at the same time firmly situating those worlds within their broader social context(s)' (Jenkins, 1984).

10.5 INTO THE FIELD

The nurses on my research ward knew me as a lecturer on a degree course in nursing in a local higher education institution, and some had met me before as I had gone about my usual roles as clinical teacher to the BSc students and occasional lecturer in the school of nursing. They had been given a copy of the research proposal, knew that hospital managers supported it, and that the ward sister had volunteered the ward for the project.

On my first day on the ward I arrived in my uniform, wearing a 'research nurse' badge instead of my usual 'nursing lecturer' badge. I introduced myself to the others present at 'report' and joined in listening to the handover from the previous shift. My main objective at this stage was to get to know people and their ways of working, and to become accepted as a nurse member of the ward team rather than being an outsider who had come to 'do research on' them.

For the first few shifts I planned simply to join up with one of the trained staff and follow them around, helping them with whatever they were doing and talking to them about their work as we went. This caused a little discomfort at first, and people often asked me what I was doing. I replied in a completely open way and this seemed to satisfy them at least somewhat. I made a point in those early days of working with all trained staff, including the enrolled nurse, because she was a permanent member of the team and I wanted her to be as involved in the project as the registered nurses. In Lathlean's study only registered nurses had been involved in the development project but this seemed unrealistic and unreasonable in a nonteaching hospital situation, particularly as my work took place at a time of insecurity for ENs as a result of Project 2000 and its consideration of the possible future demise of the EN.

When I started working on the ward I was beset by various doubts and insecurities. Would staff accept my presence or would they feel suspicious and uncomfortable, so that I could not relate to them, and change their behaviour because of my presence? Would I be able to get involved in carrying out care without feeling threatened and inadequate, and without threatening those with whom I was working, because of my status? Would

I be able to handle the physically heavy nature of the work? Would people confide in me and talk freely about their feelings and opinions? In the event all these fears proved unfounded, but other feelings came to take their place.

10.5.1 Self-doubts

Self-doubts about my ability to handle the technical and physically demanding nature of the work were soon dissipated, although not without some bravado and hidden panic! I varied my activities from just following a particular person about and observing their work, to simply joining in with trained staff and learners alike to share the work. My aim was to get to know staff as individuals and their views about the ward, to get a 'feel' of the quality and quantity of the work, and to build up my 'ward cred' to help progress in this early phase and for the 'action' phase of the project which would come later.

So when someone put their head out from behind the curtains and asked for help, I went over and offered myself if I was free. The request was usually for aid with turning or lifting a heavy patient, and my desire for acceptance overcame fears about my ageing and feeble body. Nobody seemed to notice any inadequacies, and sometimes people – especially learners – specifically asked me to help them or show them how to do something. As my confidence grew and relationships were built up, I also volunteered information or initiated a discussion both at report time and while actually carrying out nursing care. This seemed the most natural and least 'interfering' thing to do, since they all knew I was a nurse teacher. It would probably have appeared more strange had I not done so. In fact it was a patient who once noticed my awkwardness and explained to me how to work his feeding cup by holding a finger over the airvent to control the flow. On another occasion when I was feeding him he remarked that I was getting better at this and would be 'all right given time'!

As time passed and I felt I was becoming accepted on the ward, I decided that preserving the naturalness of the setting required me to behave in the way that the nurses would expect me to behave. For example, if a discussion arose at report and others were giving their opinion then I should do so too; and if a technical question arose about which I had some potentially useful information, then I should share this with the nurses. As I began to do this they did not appear to find it odd or an intrusion, and it also gave me the opportunity to ask questions for clarification when I was not clear about what was going on. A discussion occurred once, for example, about how a patient's pressure sore should be dressed. Twice an ethical issue arose, once about whether a patient who wished to be discharged should be 'allowed' to go, and once about a doctor giving information about a patient's diagnosis to a relative without discussing it with the patient first. I joined in these discussions, giving a genuine opinion but trying especially hard to express it in a restrained rather than forceful way, because I was aware of my status as a nursing lecturer and did not want to intimidate the nurses or make them reticent about talking to me.

Particularly fruitful but nevertheless problematic exchanges took place when I went to meal breaks in the dining room with the nurses. We talked about the usual topics on such occasions – home life, news items, and what was happening on the ward. Meal breaks were therefore a time for getting to know the nurses better as individuals and sharing some feeling about our work, and it was at these times that I was aware of how I had managed to become accepted as a colleague with whom they felt free to converse without restraint.

Other ways in which they indicated their acceptance included 'letting off steam' in my presence, or confiding in me in a way which implied or overtly made a criticism of the way the ward was run. On one occasion when I was alone in the office, a learner nurse came in and exploded with 'Do you know what X has just said to me? She said, "Are you just standing around doing nothing?" '. The ward was very busy and the learner had simply stopped in her tracks to collect her thoughts before going on to the next activity. She had come into the office to make a telephone call and after ventilating her emotions to me she violently punched out the number on the telephone. No response seemed expected from me on this occasion and so I was not embarrassed. But I did feel that the fact that the learner felt able to 'let go' in my presence suggested that I had become 'part of the furniture' in the way that participant comprehension requires. A similar example occurred at the start of a shift when I was in the office waiting for people to arrive. Two learners came in, looked at the off-duty rota on the wall, and one of them remarked. 'Oh good, X is not on duty today or tomorrow'.

This acceptance, therefore, was also a source of difficulty, in both methodological and ethical senses. The longer I worked on the ward the more I became aware that there were difficulties in relationships between staff, and it was at meal breaks that these problems were discussed openly among them and with me. Meal breaks therefore became a rather stressful and demanding time for me, as I sought to be a sympathetic listener but not to collude in criticizing other individuals who were not there to speak for themselves. I certainly did not feel that I should take sides, because I was only hearing one perspective and because I needed to maintain relationships with all the ward team and become a neutral facilitator for the 'action' phase of the project. If I had followed textbook advice and simply nodded and said 'uh, huh, is that so?', the nurses might have thought that I was not concerned with what they were saying or even that I was 'on the other side'. Conversely, it was clearly inappropriate to collude in the discussion and appear to take their sides. The precarious strategy I adopted was to listen, make as few comments as possible while the discussion was in progress, and when an intervention from me seemed called for I tried to introduce a constructive perspective by asking how they thought things could be done in a different way in order to improve matters. This was not always easy, and I am not sure that I always succeeded in maintaining my desired neutrality.

Another mark of my integration into the ward team was an invitation, after 2 months of working a weekly shift, to join staff at a local restaurant one evening for a staff nurse's leaving party. This party also provided fruitful information which could contribute to understanding the dynamics of the ward – for example, who sat with whom, who talked to and about whom when others could not hear, what was said, and the focus and content of jokes.

My presence certainly did have an influence on proceedings, in some ways of which I was aware and which were intended to be part of the process of building up relationships in preparation for the action phase of the project. Doubtless it had other effects of which I am unaware, but staff would certainly have been analysing what I did and said and drawing conclusions from this in the same way as I was doing as part of the research.

10.6 PERSONALITY CLASHES AND COMMUNICATIONS PROBLEMS

During this initial phase of the project, nurses often discussed the problems of the ward in terms of personality clashes and communication difficulties, and these themes recurred in the questionnaires and interviews I conducted as part of the methodological triangulation discussed earlier. Because the ward workload was heavy, I went on a number of Sunday afternoons when things were more slack in order to conduct interviews while staff were on duty. The interviews were carried out in a private room off the ward corridor to ensure confidentiality, and questionnaires and interviews were anonymous. Learners completed a ward learning environment questionnaire (Fretwell, 1982) and trained staff filled in a stress questionnaire (Hingley, 1986).

Learners completing the ward learning environment questionnaires felt that there was a great deal to learn on the ward but they were hampered in doing so by lack of staff and a heavy workload. They felt that high standards of patient care were maintained on the ward, with individualized care being given, but that the teaching they received was minimal. The main causes of stress were given as too little time to give care and for trained staff to answer questions. This led to feelings of frustration, worry and irritability. One learner wrote that 'students should get more credit – the ward can't be run without them'.

After each learner had completed the questionnaire I put it away and had a conversation, taking no notes at the time but writing down the main points that I could remember as soon as the learner had left the room.

During these conversations, many remarks were made which contradicted responses on the questionnaires. It seems likely that learners feared that what was written down could be 'used in evidence against you,' and this is probably not surprising in view of my status *vis-à-vis* the learners. I learned from these informal interviews that the ward had 'a reputation' for being heavy and disorganized, and that there were 'personality clashes' among the trained staff which caused stress. Communications were felt to be poor, resulting in learners not knowing what was happening to their patients. Learners also felt a sense of foreboding when they learned they were allocated to the ward for a placement.

Trained staff completed a stress questionnaire (Hingley, 1986), and a similar informal conversation took place afterwards. Items on the questionnaire causing little or no stress included bereavement counselling, having to perform tasks outside one's competence, coping with new technology, involvement with life and death situations, and dealing with relatives. High stress areas were trivial tasks interfering with the professional role, shortage of essential resources, and having too little time in which to do what was expected of one.

10.6.1 Disagreements

Disagreements were noted among staff in their endorsement of the statement 'Decisions or changes which affect me are made "above" without my knowledge of involvement', and this constituted one possible source of 'personality clashes' and 'communication difficulties'. Further evidence of these emerges from the informal conversations, in which staff mentioned lack of support from senior staff, with stress or difficulties being noticed but not followed up. Staff nurses did not feel they were gaining the management experience they had hoped for on the ward, and there was a marked dissonance in people's expectations of how nurses should behave and relate to each other at work. Consequently there was stress and dissatisfaction among learners and trained staff alike, and the unsatisfactory atmosphere was attributed to personality clashes, which led to communication difficulties.

Another aspect of personalities and communications mentioned by trained staff was a rigid hierarchy in the ward, with what they considered undue deference being accorded to doctors. This resulted, for example, in doctors interrupting patients' meals to examine them, and frequent interruptions to trained staff carrying out nursing work such as drug rounds.

In this project there is a clear link between the 'personality clash' theme and Pembrey's claim that the ward sister is 'the key to nursing' (Pembrey, 1980), which is another theme identified during the project. Pembrey is only one of the many researchers to highlight the key role of the sister in fostering a constructive working atmosphere and learning environment wards (see Menzies, 1960; Revans, 1964; Orton, 1981; Fretwell, 1982; Ogier, 1982).

The way learner and trained nurses described their feelings and experiences of working in the ward closely mirror this previous work, which identifies good interpersonal relationships, teamwork, individualized care and concern for learning needs as criteria of good learning environments.

10.7 IMPLICATIONS FOR THE ACTION PHASE OF THE PROJECT

The major point emerging from the observations, questionnaires and interviews is that the priority areas to work on in the action stage of the project are interpersonal relations and team building. Until staff are able to work together comfortably there will be no point in trying to introduce primary nursing, develop more comprehensive care plans or any of the other potential areas for change. Indeed a collaborative and supportive atmosphere is the essential foundation for motivation and commitment to change. The role of the action researcher as facilitator and support will be crucial, as will be relationships built up in the early stages.

Ward staff inevitably found this initial phase of the project stressful. It is discomforting to be observed at work, especially by someone of a higher professional status, even when assurances about confidentiality have been given. These need to be tested out in practice and it is even more important for an action researcher than for other kinds of researcher to be scrupulously careful about confidentiality in order to maintain participants' security and confidence for the change phase.

Susman and Evered (1978) point out that the action researcher establishes conditions for the development of others and is necessarily part of the data she helps to generate. I have discussed my role as a data generator and the strains and dilemmas which it produced for me. Another lesson which emerges clearly is the need to provide support for the researcher in the form of a confidante and mentor. Sometimes a researcher simply needs someone with whom she can 'let off steam' and be assured that confidentiality will not be broken. She also needs a research colleague, who may or may not be the same person who provides emotional support, who can discuss the research, offer insights into its processes and data, and validate the researcher's work.

10.8 CONCLUSION

In this report I have discussed the antecedents of both action research and the project. My aim has been to convey how an action researcher and her collaborators may experience action research, and to identify not only the richness of experiences and data which can result but also to focus on some of the methodological and ethical issues. I remain firmly committed to action research as a potentially fruitful way to introduce and evaluate innovation in nursing.

Acknowledgements

I would like to thank the nurses who participated in the project for their tolerance, forbearance and willingness to share their work with me. I am also grateful to my confidantes, who listened patiently to me in both my more and less rational moments.

POINTS FOR DISCUSSION

Christine Webb's seminar expanded upon a number of major themes outlined in her paper first published in the *Journal of Advanced Nursing* (1988) In particular, she focused on the issue of the involvement and cooperation of ward staff in the change process. The relationship between the action researcher and the ward leader is crucial, and one must not mistake lack of resistance to change as an indication of any positive commitment to embracing new ideas.

The first question raised by the group related to the difficulties of obtaining funding and support for action research. This brought the discussion back to well rehearsed arguments concerning the bias towards quantitive research methodologies. That action research ostensibly focuses on processes rather than outcomes was seen as one argument that made funding difficult. Also, from a methodological point of view there was still debate regarding the validity and reliability of some action research studies.

Webb argued that each of these issues could be addressed satisfactorily. For example, it was incorrect to say that action research could not begin to look at the outcomes of patient care. First, it depended upon the point in time one used to define when a process ceased to be a process activity and became an outcome. An illustration came from one participant who stressed this point, namely in a particular action research cycle carried out on a medical ward where the researcher and staff were exploring medical and nursing behaviour during ward rounds. When, through the process of elucidating activities and analysing actions both the medical and nursing staff changed aspects of their behaviour, would one call that a process event or an outcome? Of course, the answer rests on how one has defined outcome in the first place, and particularly how capable one is of specifying measurable goals (outcomes) for identifiable interventions (processes).

The questions then moved on to explore the relationship between action research and the generation of new knowledge. Is action research truly testing theories as they relate to practice or is it testing what has been written about implementing change? This particular question returned the group to considering the different orientations of research methodologies. In the traditional, positivistic sense, theories are indeed tested when all other (social and behavioural) variables are controlled. Action research does not start at this point at all – in fact, it uses the activities generated by change to elucidate theories and patterns which might well turn out to be the basis of a theory. Equally importantly, it is the interpretations of all of those who have been involved in the process that are the test of the accuracy of the theoretical analysis. A final point was made concerning how action researchers can keep their eye on where they are going. The short answer was that sometimes they would certainly not know where they were going, and only when they had reached a certain point would they be able to understand what had been happening.

REFERENCES

Bell, C. and Roberts, H. (1984) *Social Researching. Politics, Problems and Practice,* London, Routledge and Kegan Paul.

Binney, A. (1986) Primary nursing. Structural changes. *Nursing Times* 83 (39), 36–37.

Collins, H. M. (1984) Researching spoonbending: concepts and practice of participatory fieldwork, in *Social Researching. Politics, Problems and Practice,* (eds C. Bell and H. Roberts) London, Routledge and Kegan Paul.

Elliot, J. and Ebbutt, D. (1983) *Action Research into Teaching for Understanding: a Guide to the TIOL Project,* London, Schools Council Publications.

Fay, B. (1975) *Social Theory and Political Practice,* London, Allen and Unwin.

Fretwell, J. (1982) *Ward Teaching and Learning,* London, RCN.

Giddens, A. (1974) *Positivism and Sociology,* London, Heinemann

Glaser B. G. (1978) *Theoretical Sensitivity. Advances in the Methodology of Grounded Theory,* San Francisco, University of California Press.

Greenwood, J. (1984) Nursing research: a position paper. *Journal of Advanced Nursing* 9, 77–82.

Hingley, P. (1986) *Stress in Nursing,* Chichester, Wiley.

Horsley, J., Crane, J., Crabtree, M. K. and Wood, D. J. (1983) *Using Research to Improve Nursing Practice. Conduct and Utilisation of Research in Nursing,* New York, Grune and Stratton.

Hunt, M. (1987) The process of translating research findings into nursing practice. *Journal of Advanced Nursing* 12, 101–110.

Jenkins, R. (1984) Bringing it all back home: an anthropologist in Belfast, in *Social Researching Politics, Problems, Practice* (eds C. Bell and H. Roberts), London, Routledge and Kegan Paul.

Ketterer, R. F., Price, R. H. and Politser, E. (1980) *The Action Research Paradigm: Evaluation and Action in the Social Environment,* New York, Academic Press.

Lathlean, J. and Farnish, S. (1984) *The Ward Sister Training Project,* Nursing Education Research Unit, Dept of Nursing Studies, Kings College, London.

McCormack, T. (1981) Good theory and just theory. Towards a feminist philosophy of social science. *Women's Studies International Quarterly* 4, 1–12.

Menzies, I. (1960) A case study in the functioning of social systems as a defence against anxiety. *Human Relations* 13, 95–121.

Ogier, M. (1982) *An Ideal Sister,* London, RCN.

Orton, H. D. (1981) *Ward Learning Climate,* London, RCN.

Pembrey, S. (1980) *The Ward Sister–Key to Nursing,* London, RCN.

Reid, N. (1985) *Wards in Chancery,* London, RCN.

Revans, R. W. (1964) *Standards for Morale. Cause and Effect in Hospitals,* Oxford, Nuffield Provincial Hospitals Trust.

Sparrow, S. (1986) Primary nursing. *Nursing Practice* 1 (3), 142–148.

Susman, G. and Evered, R. (1978) An assessment of the scientific merits of action research. *Administrative Science Quarterly* 23, 582–603.

Towell, D. and Harries, C. (1979) *Innovation in Patient Care: An Action Research Study of Change in a Psychiatric Hospital,* London, Croom Helm.

Willmott, P. (1975) *Use of Action Research in Developing Urban Policy*, Report of a Colloquium held by the Department of the Environment. London, Department of the Environment.

Index